WHEN THE ROBIN STOPPED BOBBING

Charlton's Journey From Old Trafford to Oldham

Daniel Macionis

authorHOUSE®

AuthorHouse™ UK Ltd.
500 Avebury Boulevard
Central Milton Keynes, MK9 2BE
www.authorhouse.co.uk
Phone: 08001974150

© 2009 Daniel Macionis. All rights reserved.

No part of this book may be reproduced, stored in a retrieval system, or transmitted by any means without the written permission of the author.

First published by AuthorHouse 11/9/2009

ISBN: 978-1-4490-3152-7 (sc)

This book is printed on acid-free paper.

For Mum, Dad and Hannah.

Chapter 1

END OF AN INCREDIBLE ERA

When you support a club like Charlton, a win is always something to savour. Three points are never guaranteed, and most weeks you go to the ground more in hope than expectation. For the years when Charlton were in the Premiership, we would usually win between ten and fourteen games a season. That works out to be one win in every three or four; therefore, a win is always extra special.

When Charlton win at home, it can make the walk up the hill from the Valley seem like a breeze, even for someone without Premier League athleticism. A win can shape your weekend. There is no sense of dread when waiting for Match of the Day or Championship highlights, and the Sunday newspaper reports are something to look forward to reading. Unfortunately, in recent years, the walk from the Valley has felt more like a trek up a mountain, and three points have become a very rare occurrence.

Relegation can change you as a football fan. The Valley is an awful place to be during some games, especially when as early as half-time you know you'll lose. I would not go as far to say watching your team struggle week after week can make you depressed, but when you travel a long way to see a loss, it does seriously affect your moods. Being close to the bottom of the league can test many fans' loyalties. Certainly some have given up and deserted Charlton. However, 'thousands remain, and they'll be back next season in fine voice hoping for a promotion that will start to repair the last three years.

After years of success in England's top division, things are looking precarious for Charlton, especially with the financial crisis and the resulting struggle for many clubs to stay in business. Two relegations in three years have meant, after frequent trips to Old Trafford and Anfield, we now face weekly trips to Yeovil and Gillingham. Not so long ago the Valley would be packed full, but in the last few games of our Championship stay, there were numerous blocks of empty seats, and the ground had an even more depressing feel to it.

Charlton as a club are famous for nearly going out of business in the late '80s, playing at Upton Park and Selhurst Park and having our own fans cleaning up the Valley to make it possible for us to return and play there. The return was made possible only by the fans, and it is this that makes Charlton such a special club. In the dark days of the late '80s, Charlton never fell below the second tier of English football. Not saying things are worse now, but with Charlton being a victim of the recession and the possibility of administration and a points-deduction thing; it is hard to be too positive.

Of course, it's hard to estimate how serious the financial situation is, but with Charlton selling their training ground and with similar-sized clubs such as Southampton really struggling, it is frightening to think how bad things have got. However, I have no intention to give up on my team. I genuinely believe that no matter what level of football we play at, I will not stop following Charlton. I started to support Charlton for one reason: they were the closest team. There were plenty of choices for me living near to London as I was, and the fact that a lot of people at school followed Manchester United or Liverpool. But Charlton seemed the best choice if I ever wanted to go and watch my team.

The start of the decline culminated in Charlton being relegated to the Championship in 2007, and it hurt like hell. It was the first relegation I truly experienced as a Charlton fan. Everything I had heard and read about an unsuccessful battle was true: being near to the bottom of the league week after a week and the prospect of trips to places that may seem to have had an air of romance to an English football fan. But the reality is somewhat different (teams such as Scunthorpe and Hartlepool come to mind). I am sure the pressure for teams doing well is tough, but surely it is a lot worse at the bottom of the leagues as there is far more worry and more to lose – not only status but also players, staff and maybe, most important, money.

Nevertheless, as someone who not only follows Charlton but also the rest of the football league, I believe there was always the possibility that relegation would occur sometime. This may seem quite downbeat, but for many years it was evident Charlton were punching above their weight in the Premiership. Although it was fantastic to see us competing with top teams such as Tottenham and Aston Villa, when there are teams such as Man City and West Ham yo-yoing between the divisions, it would not be long before things would not be so comfortable. Especially when the legendary Alan Curbishley left in 2006, and for the first time in year a new era was upon the club. Never, however, was it foreseeable that things would start to go so drastically wrong.

At the time of my first match, Charlton had just started out on their incredible journey towards the top flight. I do not remember too much about the actual game, but it was against Wolves (April 1998) at the Valley under the floodlights. I know Charlton won 1–0 and 'Super Clive' Mendonca scored the winner, but aside from that, it is a hazy memory.

In April 1998 Charlton were in the running for automatic promotion from the old Division One, and the match actually was important. My dad was not a huge football fan at the time either, but I think this particular game, albeit not a classic, changed his views on football as well. He has told me his first match was at Stamford Bridge between Chelsea and Manchester United in the '60s, but he was too small to see anything and did not at all enjoy it. It is quite extraordinary to think his first match may have included George Best and Bobby Charlton. Fortunately my first football ground experience was completely the opposite.

Ultimately Charlton settled for the playoffs and were involved in one of the best games ever at Wembley, winning 7–6 on penalties after a 4–4 draw to gain promotion. I regret that I did not see us at Wembley and had become a fan a little too late to really enjoy what had gone on. Nowadays, I am not sure if I would enjoy this type of game so much. In 1998 when football was new to me, the pain of a loss was not nearly in the same league as it is now, so watching Charlton fight back from a goal down on three occasions would have been exciting. Now the bug has truly bitten, to see Charlton fall behind three times at Wembley and then win a penalty shootout would be an emotional rollercoaster.

In 1998 it was also difficult to fully understand what getting to the Premiership meant for Charlton. After nearly going out of business ten years previously to be in the top flight was quite amazing for the people of Charlton who had suffered so much. Having seen Hull City and Burnley reach the Premiership through the playoffs in the last two seasons, their journeys too were astonishing.

The first season I really started to follow Charlton regularly (1998–9) we were actually relegated from the Premiership; however, I was a bit too young to really feel the pain of relegation. Don't get me wrong; even as a ten-year-old I remember watching *Soccer Saturday* and feeling very upset when we went down on the last day. Nevertheless, on a purely selfish point of view, the fact we were playing in Division One meant there would be more opportunity to see them play (it was almost impossible to get tickets in 1998–9). And so it proved the following year was to be the first time I saw my team play constantly and felt I became a true fan. It was the start of a lifelong relationship. OK, twelve years to date, but I have no intention of leaving. Looking back, the next few seasons seemed to fly by but included some astonishing results.

Unfortunately, like many Charlton fans I don't think I quite appreciated how special these top-flight years and results were. Maybe it is an age thing, but for me Charlton getting to the 'magic forty points' often by the end of February was taken for granted, and the games and sometimes wins against the big teams were not savoured as much as they should have been. For example, coming from 3–1 down to Manchester United to draw and beating Arsenal 4–2 at Highbury for me particularly stand out. By 2006 even Curbs said there was no longer the buzz about the Valley when the big teams visited, and if we earned a point or a win it would not be a huge shock.

The draw against Man Utd was at a time when they were halfway through winning their third title in a row. Despite a good start to the game, United were ruthless in taking a 3–1 lead. Their second goal could have been one of the most famous in Premier League history: Ryan Giggs shot from the halfway line, similar to Beckham in 1996 against Wimbledon, but he hit the bar, and Ole Solskjaer scored the rebound. Alan Curbishley recently said in an interview that whenever one of the top teams played us, they rarely rotated their top players and always knew they were in a game. This game was no different as all the big guns from United played – Keane, Giggs, Beckham and the rest. This was the first time I had seen United play, and it was no big surprise when, with fifteen minutes to go, we were struggling. Ryan Giggs especially was almost unplayable at times with his marauding runs down the left wing.

However, with two goals in ten minutes, we salvaged an unlikely point, the equaliser greeted with jubilant celebrations (every Charlton fan can recollect John Robinson going mental after sweeping the ball in); and even though only a draw, it felt like a win. One of the things that also stands out from this game is when it was 3–2 to United and we were chasing. I remember my dad saying that there was no disgrace in losing to them by one goal as they were by far the best team in the country. This was true of course, but it was a great game to watch, and we fully deserved a point.

The win against Arsenal was even more unbelievable. This was during their title-winning season of 2001–2, and again all their top names played. On a personal level, this was an interesting experience as I sat with the Arsenal fans in the North Bank at Highbury. Having my lucky shirt hidden underneath a jacket and pretending to be happy when we conceded was awkward at best.

Arsenal started the match brilliantly and could have been three– or four–nil ahead but managed only the one. Somehow Charlton scored two goals, both from set pieces. The second goal was an awful own goal from Richard Wright. I don't know how my dad or I managed to keep quiet; maybe the angry home fans stopped us from anything more than a quick smile. One particular fan was very angry with his side. Normally this would have been understandable, but Arsenal had actually been playing very well and had played some superb football going forward. They were shell shocked, but despite trailing at half-time, there was the high probability that Arsenal would come out all guns blazing and normal service would be resumed. Surprisingly enough, though Charlton came out and started to dominate the game, Claus Jensen scored an audacious chip to put us 3–1 ahead before Euell came through to give Charlton a surreal 4–1 advantage.

The only downfall was that I was not in amongst the jubilant travelling fans, and I had to keep quiet. Thierry Henry pulled one back from a very debatable penalty (hard to moan about such a decision after a win like that) which raised one or two nerves with twenty-odd minutes to go; but no comeback materialised, and we had a famous win. Both of these games were released on video and later DVD, but to be there was very special.

The Arsenal win was during a season when by March we were unbeaten in London derbies and had the best record against our rivals. Arsenal had a phenomenal season, but our record for local games was better. It is quite extraordinary to think we did the double over Spurs and Chelsea as well as the win at Highbury.

There were of course other famous results, such as doubles against Liverpool and Chelsea. During the summer months Sky Sports often show season highlights, and these matches and results often feature. It almost reached the stage when these were not seen as such great shocks and matches against Charlton, for the bigger teams were seen more than just potential banana skins.

The Valley has undergone a huge transformation. As mentioned previously, the stadium was unplayable in the '80s but is now an all-seater modern ground. New stadiums are sometimes criticised for lacking tradition. Grounds such a St Marys and the Walkers may look impressive and house more supporters but lack the character of the older stadiums. Often these stadiums are miles out of town and include hotels and conference centres. The Valley has managed to achieve both the modern and traditional look. During the Premiership years, it was always near to capacity. Despite not being as intimidating as somewhere like Fratton Park or the Britannia Stadium for visiting fans and players, there is normally a cracking atmosphere.

There have been plans in place for a number of years to increase the capacity to 40,000. In 2001 the covered end was developed to incorporate another 7,000, and the plan is to make the other end similar in appearance and for all the stands to be linked. There have been planning-permission problems but the designs look exceptional, and one day it would be great to see the stadium develop even further.

As Charlton are often competing with the other London clubs for support, it is tribute to the people in charge that, through cheaper coach services and ticket concessions, the club has been able to attract fans from a wider network. South-east of London there is little option for football fans to follow a team, despite Gillingham accusing the club of pinching fans. Charlton has been able to tap into Kent and Sussex with great effect, which can only be a good thing as more people had the chance to see top flight football and we didn't have hundreds of empty seats. Gillingham may have moaned, but the majority of fans would rather watch Premiership football a get a free coach than League One, despite the distance. I'm sure, since we were last in the top flight, fans have stopped coming to the Valley in favour of West Ham or Tottenham.

Nevertheless, a lot of the success amounted to the superb management of Curbishley; throughout the years we never spent big as a club and always had a tight wage structure. There were fantastic signings as well as a great youth set up. In 2003–4 we finished seventh, which in many other seasons would have been good enough for a European place. That season Curbishley must have been a serious contender for the manager of the year. If we hadn't sold out top player, Scott Parker, in January that season, things would have been a lot better. At the time he was sold, it was not too far beyond belief that we could have mounted a serious challenge for the Champions League. The season after Everton breached the top four, and their squad and their budget were not too different from ours.

Alongside Curbs his assistant, Keith Peacock, and coach, Mervyn Day, were also part of the furniture at the club. They left with him in 2006 and would be missed. Certainly not seeing Mervyn on the touchline kicking every ball would be weird. When he left, Curbs was second only to Sir Alex Ferguson in terms of time spent as manager Fifteen years in any job is impressive but as a manager is astonishing, especially considering the ridiculous turnover of managers nowadays.

Curbishley's last season was a mixed season; ultimately a thirteenth place finish is still very commendable but having been joint top in September as well as in the European places in October, the fall away towards mid table was disappointing. The cynics will say that we started the season only so well as we played two of the promoted sides and the three teams who were eventually relegated. But to start to season with five consecutive away wins is a fine achievement. Darren Bent, whom we signed that summer, had started the season on fire, and a new 4–5–1 formation with Murphy, Smertin and Kishishev in the middle was working exceptionally well. We were the only side in Jose Mourinho's time at Chelsea to win a domestic game at Stamford Bridge, albeit a Carling Cup tie on penalties. But after this game in late October things fell away, and there were no more away wins.

Curbishley said in his autobiography that after a famous home win against Liverpool in February he did not feel the same excitement, and this contributed to his decision to question his future. I could see his point as when we were first promoted, any result against the top teams would be celebrated greatly, and sometimes we would even release a DVD of the game. By 2006 even a win against Liverpool, who were at the time champions of Europe, no longer had the same impact.

In that season we reached the quarter-finals of the FA Cup, and with the prospect of a semi against West Ham, there would have been the real possibility of a final and Europe. A home tie against Middlesbrough looked on paper like a desirable one, but their goalkeeper made some fine saves, and a replay was needed. Despite taking 5,000 fans to the Riverside, our dreams were dashed, and 4–2 flattered Boro. This was the closest we got to a final. Unfortunately the only final we may be playing in soon is the Johnstone's Paint Trophy.

Whilst in the top league, Charlton began to attract some bigger names. Danny Murphy in 2004 apparently chose the Valley over Spurs; of course this could have been to do with first team chances. But as a Liverpool player and someone with England aspirations, show that Charlton was not an unattractive option to play football. One element that worked in the club's favour is the location. London for many players is the place to be. With the greatest respect to teams and areas such as Middlesbrough, this is not the case there. Charlton may have been a smaller club within the Premiership, but in terms of getting players to want to play for us, this was never a big issue.

Paulo Di Canio was another major coup for Charlton when he signed in 2003. Despite being in the veteran stage and only staying for a year, it was great to have Paulo at the club. He scored one of the best penalties I have seen, a great chipped effort against Arsenal and helped inspire another famous 4–2 win against the billionaires of Chelsea. Di Canio will be best remembered for his time at West Ham and possibly that push on the ref for Sheffield Wednesday, but he was fantastic for us and the memory of his turning the Chelsea defence inside out before laying on a tap in for Johansson in that win is, for me, equally memorable.

Unfortunately in the press and amongst non-Charlton fans, there seems to be a school of thought that we took our position for granted. Since there has been such a decline, its serves the 'fans' right for criticising the management and wanting to be rid of Curbs when we were doing so well. However, as a true supporter I can honestly say this was not the case with the real loyal fans, the fans that were there in the late '80s when we had no ground and they had to help clean up the Valley. It was, however, the case with a small minority of fans that followed the club only when we were in the Premiership and believed we had a divine right to be there. These are the types of fans who do not truly understand football, the types who believe it is OK to boo the team when things are not actually so bad. These exist at every club.

In 2008–9 a minority of Aston Villa booed their team because they drew with Wigan at home even though their team was fourth in the league and the possibility of breaching the top four was very realistic.

In 2009–10 Charlton will be playing third-tier football for the first team in many years, and these so-called supporters will not be at the Valley getting behind the team as we try to re-build, but instead they will no doubt claim to support whoever is doing well in the Premiership. Anyway, I feel it is important to say this as if there are any non-Charlton fans reading. Then it is important to clear this up as I strongly believe – although all football fans are fickle and impatient we are nowhere near the worst offenders – Charlton as a club have rarely attracted bad press, but our fans are not always favourably looked upon. Admittedly, when in the Premiership, there was discontent when our traditional end of season slumps kicked in, but a change in management was never contemplated. This discontent was no different to that what happens at most clubs when results take a dip, but this didn't mean we as fans forgot how far the club had come and how well the team was doing.

When it was announced before a home game against Blackburn in 2006 that it would be Curbs' last game in charge, it was one of the saddest days in football. Everyone in the ground was in shock; it was so unexpected. There had been speculation in the past, and like top players he was always linked with the top jobs, notably before he left with the England job. Ironically there may be an element of regret in the FA for appointing Steve McLaren ahead of Curbishley as both were interviewed for the post.

When Curbs left, the reasons were understandable. He wasn't willing to commit longer than a year, and as a club we needed more security. Fifteen years in any job is a hell of a long time, and Curbs felt he needed a break. In his autobiography Curbs talked about the uniqueness of his departure during the second half of the Blackburn game. Everyone in the stadium stood up in admiration of Curbishley and the job he had done. Understandably Curbs looked very emotional; he wasn't the only one. He had been more than a part of the furniture at Charlton for so long.

It was clear Curbs wasn't leaving for another club, and a new era began. The reception Curbs received was unbelievable, and aside from when Sir Alex Ferguson, retires it is hard to imagine a similar scenario where a manager stays at a club for fifteen years or more and leaves with such an ovation. I have always been to football with my parents, but this particular game I was there with a friend. Immediately our thoughts turned to a possible successor. Over the summer there were numerous names linked.

One manager who reportedly was the board's choice was Peter Taylor. We were more than sceptical about this as even though he had done reasonably well at most of his clubs, the one blot on his CV was at Leicester. As we had, Leicester had enjoyed success in the premiership. Many believed this was down to their manager, Martin O'Neill. When he left, it was an almost impossible task to replace him. Taylor tried and ultimately failed as he was sacked after an awful run in the league at the end of 2000–1 and start of 2001–2. Leicester were relegated that season and have since struggled to maintain any stability. I will return to the Leicester analogy later, but when Taylor was linked there was a sense of déjà vu.

Ian Dowie, ex-Crystal Palace manager, was chosen but immediately was not the most popular choice. The Charlton Palace rivalry is not the biggest in the UK comparatively, but there is a certain edge to the rivalry. In 2004–5 our tannoy announcer was sacked for referring to them as 'Crystal Palarse' and mispronouncing their players' names in a league cup tie. This was followed by their outspoken chairman, Simon Jordan, referring to our fans as 'morons' after Charlton scored a late equaliser to effectively relegate Palace. This day was billed as Survival Sunday as any one of four sides could escape relegation. Fortunately Charlton were more than safe; but after a disappointing end to the season, we had not won for two months and were keen to end the season on a high.

On this particular day, Charlton fans celebrated and were immensely proud of this day. It may seem in bad taste to actively celebrate another team's demise, but as our nearest and dearest, what did Jordan expect? Man City effectively sent Man Utd down one year (with one of Man United's finest in the city attack – Denis Law) and no doubt they enjoyed the day. If Arsenal relegated Spurs or Newcastle to Sunderland the beneficiary would lap it up. Of course as a Charlton fan I enjoyed sending them down and even though the phrase 'what goes around, comes around' has sort of proved to be the case, it is always great to get one over on your rivals, and this was very special.

One memorable thing about the day was the Charlton fans chant 'We sent the Palace down' to the tune of the popular song 'Is This the Way to Amarillo' made famous that season by Peter Kay's *Comic Relief* track. Relations between the clubs and the chairmen were not the best, and Dowie seemed a strange choice. Even though he had done well at Oldham and Palace, he was nowhere near in the same league as Curbs. Dowie was almost the opposite of Curbishley. Dowie had been known as a motivator, someone who wore his heart on his sleeve and acted passionately on the touchline. Curbs was calmer and had the image of being a more methodical manager.

When he was appointed, there was further controversy as Dowie had resigned from Palace claiming he wanted to be nearer to his family in the north-west. Three days later, when conducting his first press conference as Charlton boss, he was issued with a writ from Palace. From being a well-run club with stability, it was already clear things would not be the same again.

I am sure Dowie was nowhere near the first choice of the fans, but when he got the job, he was our boss and needed the support of the fans. Nevertheless, for Dowie to risk legal action and leave Palace where he was well respected and had a good relationship with the fans and chairman, shows that he was committed to Charlton and serious about pushing the club to the next level.

I am sure if he had stayed at Palace or waited for an offer from another Premiership club, Crystal Palace as a club would not have felt so let down and would have welcomed him back to Selhurst Park for the work he did there. He took them from the verge of League One to the Premiership and then nearly taking them back, only for playoff heartbreak.

The board at Charlton had done a lot for the club; unlike numerous other clubs, they'd always had full support from the fans. If it was not for them, then, there may not even be a Charlton Athletic. So fans had to keep faith that the decision to appoint Dowie and then give him so much money was the best one for the club.

The end of 2005–6 was not just the end of an era at Charlton in terms of management, but also there was a massive change in playing staff. In the previous January, we had lost out legendary goalkeeper, Dean Kiely, to Pompey. In football the term *legendary* is used too often, in my opinion, but Deano deserves the tag. Over the years he earned us numerous points each season and was exceptionally dependable. Similar to someone like David James, Deano was capable of making a world-class save but unlike James, rarely made a mistake. I don't believe I am exaggerating when I say that few Charlton fans would not have swapped Deano for any other goalkeeper. In one game away against Birmingham City in 2003, he made save after save, two of which were unbelievable (headers from Dugarry and Forssell). The save from Dugarry Kiely described as his favourite career save.

Another player who falls into the legendary category is England international Chris Powell. Even though I've followed the club for only ten years, I think Powell is the best left back to play for Charlton, a true fans' favourite. I will come back to him later in the book as he returned in 2007 for a third time. Both Kiely and Powell were bought for little money and paid it back a hundred times over. Charlton have had some great goalkeepers and defenders in their history, but when discussing greatest ever teams, Kiely and Powell are rarely excluded.

In 2006 we also lost two strikers who had been at the club since we were promoted. Jonathan Johansson and Shaun Bartlett may never have been the most prolific strikers in the league. Both were worthwhile additions to the squad. J.J., for example, was on fire in his first half-season for the club and was a great finisher. Unfortunately he never recaptured that but still weighed in with a few goals and could play on the right of midfield. Shaun Bartlett also weighed in with a few goals, and if kept fit, would offer a great aerial presence. In 2004–5 he led the line well, but when Darren Bent was signed in 2005, both J.J. and Bartlett struggled to get into the side.

Lastly Jason Euell left, and despite a mixed last two years at the club, he was our top scorer three years in a row. It was rumoured Euell was on the verge of being called up by England at one point. Admittedly this was the point when Sven Goran Eriksson was handing out caps to anyone who played well for their club two games on the trot. But in a midfield role, there was a period at the end of 2002 when Euell was playing some excellent football and possibly could have added something to the squad. These players may not have been household names but never the side down and cost very little. It would have been weird starting the season with a new number one and several new faces.

The Squad that Curbs left was arguably the weakest we had for a long time. The January 2006 departures and the players released had left us short of quantity and quality. Even though the likes of JJ, Bartlett and even Chris Perry may have been past their best, they would have been valuable squad members and able deputies.

Nevertheless it was not Curbishley's job to build a squad for the 2006/07 season and the fact the squad was in a poor state only meant Iain Dowie would have to prove his worth in the market straight away. Usually when a new manager takes charge, it can take a while for him to build his own team, At Charlton, the team would be one in Dowie's image very early on.

Unfortunately after never giving Curbs much money to play with, the board decided to give Dowie a two-year budget, but it was not money well spent. Jimmy Floyd Hasselbaink was a free transfer, but as soon as we saw him in action, it was clear he was past his best, looking out of shape and a far cry from the player who struck fear into the opposition every time he had the ball in and around the box. We spent £4 million on Djimi Traore and Amady Faye, which seemed a hell of a lot for two players who were in no way going to set the world alight.

Traore, for example, had a reputation for being a bit of a donkey at the back (he is guilty of one of the funniest own goals ever in a cup tie at Burnley – it's on YouTube). Two million pounds seemed a lot for a player who, despite having a Champions League medal to his name, was not highly rated at Liverpool and was often seen as a weak link in their side. Also for years we had been blessed with England international Chris Powell in that position, who despite not being Ashley Cole in terms of his attacking qualities, is a Charlton legend and never ever let the side down had left. Surely for £2 million we could have signed someone with a bit more solidarity and less of a liability.

Amady Faye was a solid midfielder, tenacious and hard working but again wasn't going to set the world alight. One problem Charlton had was the lack of creativity in the centre of midfield. We lost Scott Parker in 2004, and even though Danny Murphy replaced his creative influence, when he left in January 2006, it was more than evident we lacked that spark in the centre, the kind of player who would unlock a defence with a single pass or had the energy to bomb up and down the pitch. Amady Faye was not the answer, and judging by Simon Walton and Omar Pouso (both Dowie signings) playing forty-five minutes for the club between them, nor were they.

Danny Murphy left for the 'bigger' club in Spurs, and despite the fact he would not be welcomed back with open arms, he was sorely missed. It seemed strange that Liverpool let him go in the first place as his undoubted quality would surely have been an asset, especially when players who didn't possess his talents were in the team the year after (Salif Diao, Biscan and Nunez). The Tottenham move didn't really work out, however. Ask any Fulham fan, and they will tell you how big his influence has been; he was instrumental in their great escape of 2008.

The last of Dowie's big money signings was a defender called Diawara. Now he had all the assets to be a top defender, but in all honesty when a defender in sunny September appears wearing gloves, you have to question whether for nearly £4 million he is up for the Premier League. Diawara eventually began to look the part towards the end of the season, but this was too late. Diawara had just been part of the Bordeaux side that had won the French League, so it is clear he is no donkey. As many foreign players do, Diawara needed time to settle. But as a fan, patience with players is difficult when your team is desperate for results.

Four million pounds is a lot of money for Charlton. When you see quality defenders who are British, you have to question the manager's policies. Jolean Lescott and Jagielka were both bought for similar money after impressing in the Championship and briefly in the top league and have since gone on the establish themselves as England squad members. Of course every manager makes transfer mistakes, even the very best (Kleberson and Djemba-Djemba at United come to mind), but Dowie was given more money than any other Charlton manager and spent it poorly.

To be fair to Iain Dowie, two signings did really work out. The first was Scott Carson, on loan for the year. Despite a lack of experience and our ultimate relegation, Carson was superb for us and looked England quality. He deservedly won our player of the year award. Unfortunately since he left, his career has been overshadowed by some high-profile mistakes. If he can recapture some of his Charlton form, he has a long time to stake a claim for England's regular. The other Dowie success was Andy Reid. Unfortunately he was injury prone in his first season but has undoubted quality and is someone who could potentially have been the creative spark we lacked. It took until the following season for this to be evident, long after Dowie left.

Alan Curbishley did not have a perfect record with his signings but had a reputation for unearthing some real gems and found some real bargains. Players such as Mark Kinsella and John Robinson were bought from the lower leagues for next to nothing but turned out to be some of our most consistent Premier League performers. Even so early into Dowie's reign, it already had appeared that if Curbs had been in charge, he would have spent the money better. In years gone by, we had signed some players, which was really exciting for Charlton (for example, Murphy and Rommedahl), but after spending so much, none of the new players fell into this category.

The squad and management had a whole new look to it; there was optimism and excitement at the club. A few pundits had predicted we would struggle; but we weren't tipped to go down, and there was a feeling that under a new management with a new squad, we could not only compete in the league but also maintain a push for Europe.

Another reason to be positive was that we had kept Darren Bent. He had been the top English goal scorer the season before and was exceptionally unlucky not to go to the World Cup. Averaging better than one in two, Bent seemed to be the missing link as he not only has pace and an aerial threat but is an accomplished finisher. Why Eriksson did not take a closer look at him is a mystery, especially as at the World Cup he opted with four strikers, two of which were not 100 per cent fit – Rooney and Owen – and the third, Walcott very inexperienced. It seemed unclear why no team had signed him before we did as for a few years he had done very well with Ipswich. It was testament to the club that we managed to stop any interest developing.

Now at Tottenham, but with an uncertain future, Bent has maintained a decent goal ratio in terms of starts to goals. Although not all Spurs fans' favourite, he is one of the best and most consistent strikers to play for Charlton in living memory. If Darren had been fit for the whole of 2006–7, there is the high probability we would have survived.

Iain Dowie had also brought back to the club Les Reed and Mark Robson. Reed was a coach in the '90s under Curbs, and Robson a decent player for us by all accounts. The new regime still had a Charlton-like feel to it. Despite reservations about Dowie's past, I think Charlton fans were willing to get behind him and believed that the future looked promising. There was the possibility of £30 million reward for staying in the Premiership in TV money and other deals; however, relegation really did not seem an option going into 2006–7.

Chapter 2

FIFTEEN YEARS AND FIFTEEN GAMES

When the fixture lists are released in June, there are always fixtures to look out for, but most important, are the early games and where vital points may be gained or lost. In the Premiership it is always important to have a decent start and get confidence levels up. In 2006 the first four fixtures – West Ham and Chelsea away, Manchester United and Bolton at home – looked at best tricky. The pessimist in me also noted that Liverpool away on the last day was not the best if we had something to play for (I was thinking Europe maybe). Unlike seasons before, there was the new-manager syndrome, so hopes remained high, as well as the fact we had never been pushovers for any team and were more than capable of a shock.

Preseason was not the best. Having a few good or bad few friendlies does not dictate the way the season will unfold, but the results and performances were not too promising. One noticeable worry going into the season, aside from the lack of a spark in midfield, was the play of the strikers. There was the prolific Darren Bent, but in terms of senior players, there was the less-than-prolific Marcus Bent and Jimmy Floyd Hasselbaink, and that was it. If Darren was unfit or off his game, there were no real options. Kevin Lisbie was still at the club but had his injury problems and had never got near double figures in a season. Also, he shared similar attributes to Darren Bent (minus the goal return), so it was unclear whether they could really form a decent partnership.

Preseason's are obviously more about fitness than form, but when you struggle to score goals against the New Zealand eleven, you have to question whether your team is good enough for the Premiership. However, it is ridiculous to start feeling negative about a season just because preseason is poor. In 2006 we also had the high turnover of players to take into account, and it takes time for them all to gel.

West Ham away on the opening day was not the easiest of starts. They had been a minute from winning the FA Cup final the previous May and had done well in the league. Dean Ashton had injured himself while away with England, which meant he was ruled out. Ashton had a good end to the previous year, and even though he has undoubted quality, injuries have hampered his West Ham and England career. Upton Park is a great ground to visit, similar to the Valley in the respect it has maintained its traditions but has been modernised to house more than 30,000 fans.

Even though West Ham could be seen as our rivals – as there are only a few miles between the clubs – there are many links between the clubs, both in terms of players and staff. If there is any rivalry, it is definitely a friendly one.

West Ham probably regard Spurs or Chelsea as their true rivals, whereas Charlton certainly include Palace as theirs. West Ham are a proper football club steeped in tradition with some true legends of the games having played for them. They have always tried to play good football, and their fans, like many others, can be impatient, but they create a fine atmosphere and really get behind their side.

Thirty minutes into the game things were going brilliantly, one goal up thanks to a Bent penalty, and playing some decent stuff. The atmosphere in the away end was cracking. Two stupid yellow cards in a matter of minutes for Traore put a dampener on things, but as we held out till half-time, there was the possibility of our hanging on for a decent result. The second of his yellows was for stopping West Ham taking a quick free kick; to say it was idiotic is a an understatement.

In the second half, West Ham were too strong, and we barely got out of our half. Two goals from Zamora, neither one great defending. And to rub salt into it, ex-Charlton loanee Carlton Cole made it 3–1. Even though the final score was disappointing, the first-half performance was good. If it hadn't been for a ridiculous sending off then, who knows? The main negatives were Hasselbaink looking slower and older and of course Traore living up to his reputation for being a liability. Still, it was onwards and upwards with Manchester United next to visit.

In all of Curbs years, we had not been close to beating United. His last game was at Old Trafford, and a 4–0 defeat was a fair reflection. But it was Dowie's first home game, and United had Rooney and Scholes suspended, so there was cause for some optimism. The suspensions were ridiculous as the two players were sent off in a meaningless preseason tournament. Even though this could have benefited Charlton, it seemed unfair to have punished players so severely and possibly cost their team vital points. Certainly if it were Charlton and someone such as Darren Bent (who was just as, if not more, important to the team than Rooney was), then we would have been more than disappointed.

This game was Christiano Ronaldo's first away game since his role in Rooney's sending off in the World Cup. Speaking as an England fan, I thinks his behaviour was despicable not just as a professional but also as Rooney's teammate. Eight years previously David Beckham had been the villain, and the fans behaviour towards him was too harsh. He made a mistake, but pictures of his being crucified crossed a line in my opinion. Beck's first away game was at the slightly more intimidating Upton Park, there is an image of him taking a corner and the home supporters reaction was unbelievable. Luckily for Ronaldo, the Valley does not have the same reputation, and the worst he got were some boos and a few crude comments. Typically as the great players do, he let the football do the talking. Beckham has since gone on to become one of England's best-loved players. Even though this won't be the case with Ronaldo, there is no doubt he is one of the world's best and is an asset to the Premier League.

As it turned out, United did not really miss them, and as in the West Ham game, after a decent first-half show, we collapsed in the second half and conceded three goals. Such a heavy defeat was no great surprise but again the manner was disappointing as their first goal was due to another individual mistake, and there was a noticeable lack of firepower and spark. Ole Solskjaer scored their third goal, his first for a few years after some horrific injury problems. If I were not a Charlton fan, I would say it was good to see such a great player back scoring. One of the most dramatic games I have seen was when Solskjaer came on and won the European Cup for United in 1999.

For the first time in years, we had started the season with consecutive defeats. Even though it is an absurd idea to publish league tables so early – as it can put unnecessary pressure on teams and managers – it is still never good to see your team near the bottom. The Bolton game therefore had extra pressure as already it felt as though we must avoid defeat and get off the mark. Yet again, though we knew Bolton would be tough, similar to Charlton, they had punched above their weight in the Premiership but unlike us, had reached Europe and could afford to spend big on players and wages. Bolton have been criticised for their style of football, especially when Sam Allardyce was there, but you have to credit how much they achieved. Allardyce managed to get the best out of players whose careers were going downhill; for example, players such as Okocha were fantastic to watch. Bolton was never an easy game, and like us they always seemed to give the top four tough games.

Our home record against Bolton was not the best; they always seemed to win at the Valley for some reason. With this in mind and after two defeats, our preseason optimism was turning into pessimism. After sixty minutes Charlton had been reduced to ten men and had a penalty awarded against them. Things seemed to be transpiring against us.

Unlike the West Ham game, we held out well. Scott Carson showed his quality with a penalty save, and Darren Bent got two goals himself, one a good link up with Jimmy. Bolton had Kevin Davies sent off for a dubious elbow, but we deserved the win and were off and running. At Palace Dowie had created an image of a team with tremendous character and team spirit. In the Bolton game, it looked as though this had carried through.

Not surprisingly the away game against Chelsea ended in defeat. But there were many positives to come from the game, especially as Charlton had made the trip across London with injuries and suspensions already taking their toll. Hreidarsson was suspended after being sent off against Bolton, and Amady Faye had to play centre half because of the injuries. Andy Reid and Diawara also limped off in the game, so for the third game out of four, we ended with ten men, this time having used all our subs.

Only a few months before we had travelled across to Chelsea and more than deserved the point we achieved. Charlton were the only domestic side not to suffer defeat at Stamford Bridge, so there was some optimism going into the game. Chelsea won 2–1 this day and deserved the points; but with our threadbare squad, it looked as though the season could be prosperous. Scott Carson saved another penalty as well as making some fine saves, and Hasselbaink finally got off the mark with a well taken goal against his former team.

A home game against Portsmouth showed our weaknesses. Pompey were doing well in the league, but the 1–0 defeat flattered us. In the first half, they could have had two or three, and we barely created anything going forward. Even with our injuries and suspensions, the performance was very poor, and four defeats out of five was not what we expected at all. The first half was Omar Pouso's first and only outing in a Charlton shirt – possibly Dowie's worst signing – and the Uruguay international was never seen again. The goal that won it for Pompey was soft. Carson could have done better, but after his performances so far it would be harsh to blame him.

During the early part of the season, across London at West Ham, there was astonishing goings on. West Ham had started the season well; but at the end of the transfer window, the Argentinean duo, Carlos Tevez and Javier Mascherano, arrived. There was no clear reason why they had gone to West Ham when, with the greatest of respect to them, the players could almost have gone to any club they desired. In the World Cup, Tevez had been involved in one of the greatest team goals seen at a tournament, this in a 7–0 win when Argentina looked genuine contenders for the cup. The transfers would later cause mass controversy, but at the time it seemed as though these players would be great additions to the Premiership and maybe give West Ham a genuine shot at challenging for the top six.

Nevertheless, as Charlton performances and results were not so great, we did not pick up another point until late October, and all the preseason optimism was disappearing. An away game at Villa was hugely disappointing as we lacked creativity and the killer finish. Villa Park was one of Charlton's bogey grounds; following a win in 1999, we had not won since. Our performances had always been sub-standard, and this time around was no different as we were beaten 2–0.

A good performance in a defeat to Arsenal did not cover up the fact that we were left at the bottom of the league, and the signings were not working out. Jimmy missed a real sitter, which would have got us a good point; a free header only a few yards out was not what the Premiership was used to from Hasselbaink. In this game Charlton were definitely the victims of an injustice. Robin Van Persie should have been sent off for a high tackle on Hasselbaink. There was no doubt this deserved more than a yellow card, but typically as the top four often do, the decision went for them. Typically Van Persie then went and scored one of the goals of the season to win Arsenal the game and to compound our misery. Gallas got away with a blatant handball, which denied us a stonewall penalty.

Leaving the Valley, I felt sick. We had not at all got the rub of the green, the referee had a real stinker and despite Carson busy in goal, we should have scored more than one. This was a very frustrating game. Charlton had perhaps played the best they had for a while but had been denied by some dreadful decisions. Supposedly these decisions are supposed to even themselves out; but when poor decisions obviously contribute so significantly to the result, it is hard to see this.

In 2002 we had a similar start to the season and found ourselves at the bottom after the ten-game point. But a noticeable difference was that in 2002 we had one or two injuries and a very difficult fixture list. When our star man Scott Parker returned, and the games against the top teams passed, things began to pick up dramatically, and we had a successful season. In 2006 there was no one to come back into the squad who would transform things, and the fixtures were not on paper as tough as they were four years before. Also in 2002 we had Curbs at the helm. Iain Dowie had yet to install confidence in the fans that he was the man for the big tussles and challenges. His only other season as a Premiership boss had ended in relegation.

Following an international break, we had an away game at Fulham on a Monday night. Again we contributed to our own downfall and left empty-handed. To make things worse, I was going to the match with a friend, Conor, and we arrived late after getting off the tube at the wrong station. We got off at Fulham Broadway, which is nearer to Chelsea's ground. As we found out, it's more than just a five-minute walk to Craven Cottage. The only positive was that we did not miss any goals.

This is why I am not a fan of away trips. I know it is bad to not always follow your team away, especially when they are in London. But away games are always significantly more expensive than home games are and always seem to take ages to get to and from. Even away trips in London are always at least twice the journey time to the Valley, and as a particularly sore loser, I find the journeys back with the other fans particularly hard. My record at away games is not the best. Rarely have I seen us win, the main exception the 4–2 win at Arsenal when I was sitting with the losing side – typical, the three away games I went to in early 2006–7 were at West Ham and Chelsea (defeats) and Fulham.

In the first half, we played well; but the defending in the second was poor, and were two goals down. Darren

Bent pulled one back, but it was too late. Even though the fans were not too despondent, there were chants of 'The Premier League is upside down'. There were one or two murmurs, and someone tried to start a chant of 'Bring back Alan Curbishley', but there was no real calls for Dowie to leave.

It was evident that up front there were serious problems. Darren Bent had carried on scoring regularly, but Hasselbaink and Marcus Bent had managed only one league goal between them. Even though personally I think the transfer window is not a bad idea, we did need some extra firepower soon or someone who would at least provide a threat to the opposition rather than the too old and too out of shape Hasselbaink or the goal- and shot-shy Marcus Bent.

The reason the transfer window is valuable because it can help stop teams' buying their way out of trouble at the bottom after January and can ease pressure on smaller clubs who are desperate to keep their better players. Of course there are people in football who believe that the transfer window leads to massively inflated prices. But surely it is assuring for teams to know the squad they have on 1 February is theirs until May rather than having their players linked with other clubs every day in the media. For the fan the transfer windows are always . In August 2008 the last night was amazing to watch as Berbatov and Robinho's transfers were unfolding. Sky Sports News is certainly the place to be as the yellow bar at the bottom of the screen is constantly updated.

Fortunately despite only one league win, we were not cut adrift at the bottom. Teams such as Watford and Sheffield United were also struggling, and safety was not too far away. It seemed as though Dowie was not under too much pressure from the fans or the board. He had barely had ten games in charge; and after fifteen years of Curbs, it was far too early to consider a change. Performances began to pick up. We deserved to beat Watford at home, but another potential England number one, Ben Foster, showed his class and earned them a 0–0 draw. This was followed by a credible 0–0 away at Newcastle when Carson made some good saves. So even though we were bottom, it seemed as though Dowie was beginning to settle.

As expected Watford and Sheff Utd were struggling after promotion. Interestingly West Ham were struggling as well. A run of defeats meant Alan Pardew was under pressure, and his job was being questioned. There were rumours that their Icelandic owner wanted his own manager. It was around this time that Alan Curbishley's name was being linked with West Ham. This was no surprise. He had grown up a fan and had played for them. The Argentinean signings were not working out, and it was clear that confidence levels were low. Another surprise was the success Reading were enjoying after promotion. It seemed Coppell had found a few real gems, and they looked a capable team not expected to be near the bottom.

Even during our bad run, there were some massive positives. Obviously Bent and Carson gad been excellent, but Andy Reid looked a real gem in midfield. He seemed to be the missing link, with clear Premier League quality. Reid may have been criticised for his shape; but we looked a better side with him in the team, and he seemed to be the creative influence we'd been missing. Reid had been very unlucky not to get on the score sheet, but some good saves and the width of a post had denied him.

In early November we finally earned another valuable home win against Manchester City, a good all round performance capped with Darren Bent (who else?) scoring the winner. Scott Carson made some fine saves; and even though we were nervously holding on at the end, the three points were deserved. As would be a constant theme throughout the season, the Charlton Web site led with a headline portraying Carson and Bent as the heroes. This was accurate and made the fans wonder where we would be without them. This game was quite special. It was the first Saturday of the season when in the second half the floodlights came on and we were attacking the covered end (think Charlton's version of the Kop).

Playing under the lights always seems to crank up the atmosphere; and this game was no different, especially as we were holding on. When looking back on this season, the Man City game was a highlight, maybe because it felt like a must win or at least a must-not lose. This was real edge-of-the-seat stuff. When the final whistle went, the relief was massive.

Man City had Nicky Weaver in goal. He had had years of injuries and was getting back to the form that earned him England U21 caps. However, at this time he was not the most popular figure at the Valley because in a Division One match in 1999, he wasted time and acted un unsportsmanlike. I was not at the match and was quite surprised by the negative reaction to him.

This would not be the last of Nicky we would see at Charlton. Another player we would soon and regularly was Ben Thatcher, who was making his first appearance since a lengthy ban after a horrific challenge on Pedro Mendes. Like Ronaldo, Thatcher, I am sure, did not feel nervous about returning to the Premiership at the Valley. As good as the Valley is for atmosphere, in terms of intimidation and hostility, many other grounds are worse to return to after controversy.

The only negative from the game was that we remained at the bottom as Watford picked up their first win of the season against Boro, and Sheffield United picked up three points. This showed how valuable the win was as otherwise there was the risk of being cut adrift. Going home after a match being stuck in traffic is also more bearable after three points. But when you hear that other results have gone against you, it does put a downer on things, but a good win and a third clean sheet on the bounce was more than a positive step forwards.

During the week we sneaked through to the quarter-final of the League Cup after beating League One Chesterfield on penalties after a 3–3 draw. A crazy game, in which Hasselbaink scored twice, could have gone either way. But the main thing was we had survived the scares to give us a shout of a cup final, especially with League Two Wycombe to play in the quarters.

The following Saturday I tuned into *Soccer Saturday* as usual, feeling cautiously optimistic about our away trip to Wigan. For years on a Saturday, if Charlton were not playing or away from home, I would be glued to the television. Even now I do find it a strange concept that four ex-footballers watching a screen and reporting on a game could be so popular and amusing, but it is and has become just as an important part of a Saturday as *Match of the Day*. The show can also prove to be immensely frustrating. The twenty seconds when you know there has been a goal in your game but you have to wait for Jeff Stelling to say which way it has gone is agony at times. It's also frustrating when you are waiting for your game to finish as all the scores seem to be coming through except the Charlton one, but when it goes your way, the ecstasy is almost the same as actually being at the game.

It is hard to recall who was reporting on the Charlton match that Saturday, but what was clear was that our defending was awful again; and despite Marcus Bent getting off the mark, another defeat was hard to take. Only a goal in the ninetieth minute made the defeat a little more respectable at 3–2. But when seeing the highlights later, and the manner of the third goal, a free header from a set piece, there were problems at the back and a long winter was in store. Diawara especially was dreadful at the back, making elementary mistakes to gift Wigan two goals by letting the ball just drift over his head.

On the Monday night, the news broke on Sky Sports that Dowie had been sacked. Shock! Horror! After Curbishley being in charge for fifteen years, Dowie had lasted only fifteen games. The timing seemed strange as we had lost only one in the last four. The board had given Dowie a two-year budget and then decided he was not the man for the job. Although not a fan of Iain Dowie when he was appointed and the fact he essentially wasted so much money on less-than-adequate players, to sack a manager without giving him a chance to truly stamp his authority on the club is ridiculous.

Iain Dowie had only twelve league games in charge; and his record, when studied further, was not so bad. We had played and lost against Chelsea, Manchester

United and Arsenal, which was almost expected, and had some awful injury problems. Two of Dowie's big-money signings – Reid and Diawara – were injured almost immediately, which summed up our luck early on. On paper our next few games looked more favourable; and with the injured players coming back, there seemed no reason for such a decision.

What made the sacking even more shocking was the legal battle occurring between Dowie and his old club Palace. Dowie had the full support of the people at Charlton, and it was clear that the club had gone a long way to appoint him a few months previously. The club could have opted for a number of other candidates with similar credentials and no legal issues, but to be so committed to Dowie and then to sack him without giving him at least a season takes some explanation.

Whether this decision was justified, only time would tell. In recent years many of the teams that have survived after poor starts changed their manager. In 2005, when West Brom staged their great escape, they had appointed Bryan Robson in the late autumn. Portsmouth the following year waited longer to re-appoint Harry Redknapp, but he masterminded their survival. The hope was that a new manager could ensure safety and maybe even a bit more with plenty of games still to play.

In the modern game, many people criticise chairmen and boards for sacking their managers without giving them a fair crack. In 2008 Blackburn, under Paul Ince, were in a similar situation to Charlton two years before, and Ince did not make it to Christmas. Paul Ince had a difficult job replacing Mark Hughes, but the situation was nowhere near impossible to change when he was sacked. I am sure the board at Blackburn feel justified as they eventually survived in the Premiership due to good form when Sam Allardyce took over. But it does not change the fact that people who run football clubs are too hasty in wanting to change and playing with managers reputations. Sometimes the people in charge think because they own a club they know and understand the game better than the managers do. We have heard rumours regarding the owners at QPR picking the team, and Mike Ashley's behaviour at Newcastle in Kevin Keegan's departure has been heavily criticised. Not saying that the board at Charlton should be too heavily criticised. Don't let's forget they helped saved the club from extinction as well as helped build up and establish us in the Premiership.

Admittedly there is now extra pressure on football club owners as the cost of relegation is so high and as has been seen with some big clubs, teams may never return, and financial ruin becomes a reality. Leeds United are a good example but are such a big club it is inevitable that they will return one day. Unfortunately the same can't be said for the likes of Southampton. This still does not excuse chairmen's actions at times. There was a time when it seemed as though buying a club was fashionable, and businessmen who had no real knowledge of the game thought they could get involved with football politics. Randy Lerner at Aston Villa is an example of how a chairman should act. He maybe does not have the football past of someone like Niall Quinn, but he has given good financial support to Martin O'Neill and has not interfered with the playing side. Instead he is seen at grounds giving his support, and there are no rumours of his signing his own players or wanting to pick the team.

Since leaving Charlton, Dowie has struggled to repeat the job he did at Palace. At the end of 2008–9 he was part of Newcastle's relegation from the Premiership. Even though you cannot blame him for this as Newcastle is a club with massive problems, Dowie's reputation has not improved since 2006. Dowie is still a good manager who may well still prove himself in the top flight; however, his record in the transfer market is poor and has been a major factor in two Premiership relegations.

Thoughts again turned to Dowie's successor. Controversially I was in favour of someone like Graeme Souness because he is not everyone's cup of tea and has not always enjoyed great success (a friend of mine says he is the reason for Liverpool's decline in the '90s). I believe there is far more to it than Souness, such as changes in the game and player culture, and Liverpool, unlike Manchester United or Arsenal, struggled to adapt. I have read one or two of the Liverpool players' autobiographies who were there in the '90s, and it seems as though any manager would have struggled to repeat the success of the '80s at Liverpool.

Souness remains well respected in the game and was the kind of character we needed. He had done a very good job at Blackburn (a similar size club to Charlton) by getting them promoted and then into Europe. Even though Dowie had achieved some good things when with the club, apparently he played a major role in persuading Darren Bent to stay with the club when he could have left to join a 'bigger' club. He ultimately struggled to replace Curbishley. There was a need for a strong character who would not be fazed trying to replace such a legend. When Martin O'Neill left Celtic after much success in 2005, Gordon Strachan was exactly the type of character they needed. Strachan was not everyone's choice, but you cannot argue with his record. There and this is an example Charlton should have followed.

If Dowie had gone two weeks earlier, Alan Pardew's name would have been linked; but West Ham had a mini-revival, beating Blackburn and Arsenal at home, so it seemed at this point as though he would be staying. Alan Curbishley understandably was loosely linked with the post, but he was quick to rule it out. It would have been great for him to return, but they do say never go back. There were obviously other names mentioned, but the choice the board went with was even more ludicrous than Dowie: his assistant, the untried Les Reed!

Chapter 3

LES MISERABLES

Les Reed was a Charlton man. He had been Curbs' assistant when we were promoted in 1998 and had fantastic credentials as a top coach. The only man to have coached England at every level of international football– including seniors during Kevin Keegan's tenure – Reed was obviously very highly regarded as a coach and had done well with England youth sides. When Dowie was sacked, most fans assumed Reed would be the caretaker until we could find a worthy successor; instead the board gave him the job full time. This meant he was now seen as Curbishley's long-term successor, someone who had never managed a club before now had the task of keeping us in the top flight.

I think most Charlton fans were in shock at this appointment. There were some rumours about Reed playing a role in Dowie's sacking to get the job for himself, but this was not really the issue. This season survival in the top league meant even more as there was the promise of even more TV money and revenue. Figures such as

£30 million were talked about when assessing the reward for staying in the Premiership. This could explain why Dowie received so much money. But with this is mind, surely Charlton needed to ensure that the man to keep us up was experienced and knowledgeable about the Premiership. People such as Souness, O'Leary and Hoddle had been there and done it and were also the kind of big names that would help to attract the big-name players and get the club back on track.

One big worry aside from the lack of experience was that Les Reed was an interior appointment. In modern-day football, interior appointments do not work, especially when managers are fired or leave under a cloud. There is need for a new manager with new ideas and a new regime. There was no doubting Les Reed was a good coach, but good coaches do not always make good managers. Some are more suited to being number twos or staying in the background. Steve Wigley at Southampton was a good example of someone who is probably more suited to coaching and struggled to have the same success as a manager. Over the years many interior appointments have failed, notably Steve McLaren with England, Tony Adams at Portsmouth and even Grant at Chelsea.

Despite off-the-field problems, Sven Goran Eriksson had done well with England in my view. We qualified for every major tournament with relative ease and always reached the quarter-finals. Even though the performances in the last eight were not brilliant, reaching the quarter-finals of a major tournament is still a decent achievement for England. We are not the best side in the world but are in the top five to eight. Unfortunately technically England are still behind the likes of Brazil and Italy. We have tremendously talented individuals but need to learn to play as a team. Now under Fabio Capello, we are starting to gel as a team and look capable of competing with the world's best, but this does not happen overnight.

Sven may have made mistakes – the second half against a ten-man Brazil in 2002 when we barely threatened to equalize and taking only four strikers to Germany in 2006 (Owen and Rooney not 100 per cent fit and an untried seventeen-year-old Walcott). But how can we forget beating Germany 5–1 on their own patch and beating Argentina in 2002. When he took over in 2000, things were not looking too positive for the national sport. An inept showing at Euro 2000 highlighted this and one point from two qualifiers against Germany and Finland. In 2006 we had a team that included the world's best midfielder, Steven Gerrard, and potentially one of the best players in Wayne Rooney. Ferdinand and Terry are not bad defenders either.

Sven did not leave in the best circumstances, and England needed a new man with fresh ideas. Hiring his assistant McLaren when there were better candidates (including Curbs and Capello) was a mistake.

The people in charge at Charlton let the fans down with the appointment of Reed. If those in charge believed that things would not improve under Dowie, and he was not the man, there remained more than half the season to salvage things. The next few league games with Reed in charge made the task of staying up much harder.

After the initial shock, again we had to get behind the team and hope for the best. Reed's first game in charge, away at Reading, was difficult but still very much winnable. For the second Saturday in a row, watching

When The Robin Stopped Bobbing

Sky Sports was not a pleasant experience as the reporter describing the game said that we were outplayed and Reading fully deserved their 2–0 victory. Yet again there was no new-manager syndrome and no change. Fortunately results did not go against us very much, so, even though we were still bottom, we were not too far adrift. Watching the post-match interview with Reed, I worried about his lack of charisma. He did not look or sound like a football manager, and it was difficult even at this stage to have confidence in him. Compared to Dowie, who seemed to kick every ball on the touchline and had the exterior of someone who really cared, Reed did not have the same personality.

Clearly there was a problem with the players. We had some good wingers and creativity from the wide areas, but even here there were weaknesses. Dennis Rommedahl was probably the quickest player in the Premiership and had bags of ability but did not have the consistency or the stamina to be able to cope with the Premiership week in week out. I thought he was a great asset that should have been utilised better. Defenders and fullbacks hate playing against pace and trickery, but we did not use him well enough. Rommedahl did score a winner in the ninetieth minute at Crystal Palace; for this alone he will be remembered fondly. Also on the wing was the undoubted talent Jerome Thomas. Not fancied by Arsene Wenger at Arsenal he still had the potential to be on the league's best wingers. He was blessed with good pace and trickery, but unfortunately consistency and final delivery often proved a problem for Jerome. Although on his day he could change a game, often it was frustrating to watch.

In the centre there was still a lack of creativity and there became a problem with Andy Reid. Again, he has undoubted talent, but aside from weight and injury issues, there was also a problem regarding his best position. Not blessed with enough pace to play on the wing, and possibly not quite strong enough or have to engine to play in the centre, it seemed to me that his best position was either just off the main striker or in the centre in a three-man central midfield, where his strengths would be best utilised.

Finally up front there was still no goal return from anyone, apart from Darren Bent, which was a worry. After seeing Hasselbaink continue to score one in two at every club before, it seemed a mystery why he could barely manage a shot in anger at Charlton. I was not really a fan of Marcus Bent. We spent £2.5 million on him, a player who may work hard but had never scored goals regularly and had had numerous clubs. Everton bought him for under £500,000 in 2004, and after seven goals in forty-four games, it seemed strange that in early 2006 his value had rocketed to more than £2 million. It was evident that no matter who the manager was, we needed a change in the playing staff or at least an upsurge in form and a bit more consistency.

Reed's first home game was against Everton in a lunchtime kickoff. Everton had done extraordinarily well and were on course for a top-six finish, so it was never going to be an easy game. Lunchtime kickoffs are great for neutral fans or fans who can't make the game. On a Saturday before going to Charlton or tuning in to *Soccer Saturday*, it is fantastic to see a live game. But if you are planning to go to the game, lunchtime kickoffs have many problems. The obvious one is the lack of atmosphere at these games; rarely does the match have the same feel as a Saturday 3 p.m. kickoff or a Tuesday night under the lights. Even the home fans have to get up earlier than usual, and it is often left to the players to wake the fans up rather than the other way around.

This Saturday game was uneventful in the first half. Everton probably deserved to be a goal up, and only Carson had saved us so far. It is often a cliché to say that certain goals and occurrences go against you only when you are near the bottom. The own goal which put Everton ahead was very unfortunate – as Carson was left wrong footed – fell into this category. Everton did not really push on, and Marcus Bent – of all people – came on and made a difference. He set up Andy Reid for a well-taken equalizer; following that, we had enough chances to win the game. Charlton could not take advantage. Conor, who was sitting next to me, said we would rue the period when we were in ascendancy. He was right. On paper a point against Everton after being a goal down was not disastrous, but because of the period after the goal, it felt as though we had dropped two points.

After the match we discussed the next few games. We felt as though the next two games were vital, away at fellow-strugglers Sheffield United away and at home to Blackburn. Six points would be a big ask, but at least three points were a must, especially with the prospect of being bottom at Christmas otherwise. There was reason for optimism. The only sides that had won at the Valley all season were near the top of the league, and performances had picked up a little in recent weeks. Talk of our being doomed seemed premature.

Charlie Nicholas was reporting on the Sheffield United away game. From this it was clear that Charlton effectively got a thrashing. Even though we took the lead from another Reid goal, from the report it seemed as though every time Nicholas described the action, it was either a bad miss or a great save from Carson. After years of *Soccer Saturday* viewing, it is easy to recognise which one of the panel is shouting. So on this afternoon every time Nicholas shouted something like 'He must score' my heart skipped a beat. Sheffield United scored two goals in the last quarter to give them a deserved victory, but it was the manner of the defeat that hurt. When reading the report afterwards, Charlton barely got out of their own half, and it could have been four or five. The defeat left us seven points behind Sheffield United; again, the only positive was that we were still in touching distance of Watford, who were not taking advantage.

Andy Reid had scored his second in two games at Sheffield United. He had excelled in Les Reed's tenure, and everything that was good about our attacking play seemed to come through him. After signing for the club in August, when has was not 100 per cent, if Reid avoided any more injuries, then surely he'd have a massive part to play.

The following Monday, the night before a vital home game against Blackburn, I was taken into hospital with a serious glandular infection. This meant there was no chance of making the Blackburn match; instead there I was lying in the hospital bed thankful for Sky Sports on the bedside TV. Amazingly we won the game in the ninety-second minute from an El Karkouri free kick. I was too ill to celebrate and could only imagine the jubilation at the Valley. Finally after three months we were off the bottom. Apparently it was a good performance, and we deserved the win. My parents did not make the match, so I could not ask them. But from the highlights on Sky, it seems Charlton had the better of it. Suddenly again, things were looking up.

Despite the win, Scott Carson made one or two fine saves to preserve his clean sheet. Even though he had a leaky defence in front of him, barely any of the goals could be attributed to his role. After winning numerous England Under 21 caps, a full cap surely could not be far away. Dean Kiely, like Curbs, had been at the club for a long while and had always been first choice, so it was fantastic to see another keeper come in and look capable of replacing him. For any club a good keeper is vital as generally he will earn a fair proportion of a team's points in a season. So far, Carson had been influential in our three wins. The only problem was that even if we survived, Liverpool would probably want him back.

The gap to the teams above was now closer, and the following night West Ham lost again. The pressure on Pardew was mounting, and rumours of Alan Curbishley becoming their next boss were beginning to circulate. Immediately there became the possible scenario of Charlton and Curbs' West Ham being involved in a relegation tussle. As football often does, the phrase 'You could not write it' came to mind. But it was far too early to be taking seriously the potential outcomes.

Despite having supported Charlton for only about twelve years, I had never seen worse than the three performances and results after the Blackburn games. I had the displeasure of being at the last two, both at the Valley. The first of this trio was away at Spurs, a humiliating 5–1 defeat. Despite being 2–1 down at half-time, and with a chance of nicking a point, a crazy spell, as described by the Web site, led to three goals against us and no way back. Jeff Stelling made a remark when the fourth goal went it about Les Reed discovering the harsh reality of Premiership management. At that point I think Stelling himself would have done a better job than Reed had done.

Normally after a game I check the Charlton Web site or any interviews shown on Sky to see what the manager's reaction is. After the Spurs game, Reed came out and in no way inspired confidence. He said the only good thing was to come out of the game was a heart-to-heart he had with the players in the dressing room. With the greatest of respect to Reed, the idea he locked the players in the dressing room and gave them a dressing down did not create the same impression that 90 per cent of the other managers do in a similar situation.

After a heavy defeat, you would want to avoid many managers.. Sir Alex is the obvious one, but most managers do have the persona that they could strike fear into most players. Les Reed still did not look or sound like a football manager, and he did not inspire great confidence. This is not always a bad thing in a manager. Sven Goran Eriksson, for example, has a similar exterior. But the difference is Sven's results speak for themselves, and he has enjoyed great success all around the world. Reed had managed us for only five games.

During the week Alan Pardew had been sacked as West Ham manager, and Alan Curbishley was appointed. It felt strange to see Curbs in another team's pressroom talking about another team, but it was always going to happen after he left. Even though West Ham were our rivals at the bottom, there was a big part of me which wanted Curbs to do well and prove he was a tremendous manager. But this raised the possibility of Pardew being the next Charlton boss if things continued. Despite the Blackburn match being a great result and restoring some faith, the Spurs match was a real setback; and with the prospect of Liverpool next, the emotions of being a football fan near the bottom of the league were being felt.

The prospect of Liverpool was even worse as Scott Carson was ineligible because Liverpool were his parent club. Nothing against our reserve, Thomas Myhre, but he was nowhere near the same class as Carson was despite being much more experienced. Myhre was wrongly in my opinion promoted to our number one in favour of Dean Kiely the year before. Even though he was a steady goalie, he still had a gaffe in his locker, in comparison to most other Premiership keepers, he was not going to earn his team as many points as others had done.

During the week there were reports in the media about Steven Gerrard not being Les Reed's biggest fan after the way Reed and a fellow coach treated Gerrard at Euro 2000. A year or so before, I had read Gerrard's autobiography and the chapter about Euro 2000. From his account it seemed as though the coaches in question could have treated Gerrard better, especially as it was his first major tournament, and he was still relatively inexperienced. Nevertheless, as has been seen on many occasions, autobiographies are not always accurate accounts and there are two sides to every story. The major worry here though was that Gerrard may now be gunning to score and prove a point to Reed even more so.

Alan Hansen on *Match of the Day* described our performance against Liverpool the next Saturday as the worst by a Premiership side he had seen. It is difficult to be sure if he was exaggerating as on paper a 3–0 reverse against Liverpool is not the worst result, certainly compared to Manchester United beating Ipswich and Nottingham Forest 9–0 and 8–1, respectively. But this game was an awful performance by Charlton, and it could have been 9–0 but for very poor finishing at times. In the first five minutes, we were a goal down to the most blatant penalty you have ever seen. Surprisingly enough, against his former club Traore was the culprit with a ridiculous high boot. Liverpool fans must have been laughing at us for spending so much money on such a donkey. The rest of the first half was unbelievably one sided. Dirk Kuyt could have had a hat trick on his own.

In the second half, it continued the same way, but amazingly enough, Charlton should have scored one maybe even two goals. Darren Ambrose missed a good chance on the volley, and Darren Bent then had an even better chance but could not steer the ball past Reina. Typically though Liverpool went up the other end and scored two goals in the last ten minutes, Gerrard – of all people – curling in a third. A point would have been one of the biggest injustices of the season as Liverpool at times were so dominant it must have felt like a practise match.

Safety was still a way off; but Watford were not capitalising, so it looked as though they would be bottom at Christmas. Sheffield United and West Ham were also not too far ahead, which was one saving grace. The day after the Liverpool game, West Ham were playing Manchester United in Curbs' first game in charge. As I sat down to watch the match on Sky, I fully expected United to ruin the afternoon for our ex=manager. In all of Charlton's Premiership years, we never got close to beating United. Not that there were not good performances, but I guess Charlton just never caught United on one of their off days. Amazingly West Ham won the game with a late winner, and Curbs had his dream start. He had an instant impact. Even though West Ham rode their luck and owed a debt to their goalkeeper, Rob Green, I think most people after the game thought that with West Ham's undoubted quality in their squad and Curbishley in charge, they would be fine.

Two days later came one of Charlton's darkest nights in the quarter-final of the Carling Cup at home to Wycombe. Despite the change of manager and poor league form, we had done well to reach the quarters; and there was the prospect of a final, especially as Wycombe were three divisions below. I know most managers would say the league is the priority, and of course it is. But a cup run can improve confidence, and a trip to Wembley, or in this year the Millennium Stadium, should not be sniffed at.

The League Cup, or Carling Cup as it is now known, is not the most respected competition, and most teams do not take it seriously until the later rounds. Nevertheless, it is a chance for the teams outside the top four to win a trophy, get into Europe and have a fantastic day out. To go to Wembley and encounter the atmosphere with 90,000 people must be an amazing experience. Fans of Chelsea or United must be used to it, but the chance to see most teams at Wembley is almost a once-in-a-blue-moon occurrence. I was not at Wembley in 1998 but would love to see Charlton at the national stadium again. In recent years, aside from Portsmouth, the FA Cup has been monopolised by the top four, whereas in the Carling Cup more teams from lower down the league have reached the final and won.

Charlton were heavy favourites going into the game, and Conor and I felt as though this was the perfect chance to restore some confidence and get a valuable win. Another worrying aspect to Reed's tenure was the lack of goals by the normally reliable Darren Bent. Obviously it is hard to criticise your best players and someone who has earned the majority of your points, but it was clear his performances had dipped since Dowie left. Apparently Bent was a big fan of Dowie and his methods. During the summer, when Bent was linked with a move away, Dowie had proved instrumental in persuading Bent to stay; so it would have been understandable if he was affected more than most by the sacking. Playing a League Two side at the Valley would seem like a great opportunity to get Bent back on the goal trail. Our captain, Luke Young, was injured, so Reed gave the armband to Bent. This seemed a clever idea to try and inspire Darren even more.

It is often said that when a team upsets the odds and wins a tie against a higher division side, it is difficult to tell who is the bigger side. In this particular game, Wycombe controlled the game, and there was no way Charlton looked a Premiership side. The goal that won the game was possibly Diawara's worst moment for Charlton as he got turned inside out by Easter, who finished well. The rest of the game was awful. Charlton never looked like scoring. But the game is perhaps more memorable for the fans' reactions. Darren Bent did not respond to the captaincy as he did not really get into the game whilst others looked almost disinterested at times. It was clear that, if we had got a result, it might have bought Reed more time. But the players did not respond and maybe did not want to save Reed's job.

I will later talk about whether booing at football grounds is acceptable and when it goes too far. This night the team were booed off, but in the second half, chants of 'You're not fit to wear the shirt' began to sound out, followed by 'Super Al, super Alan Pardew'. The board had let the fans down by appointing Reed, and even Dowie was not the fans choice. It became apparent that it was time for the board to listen. These two particular chants that rang out summed up the problems: It was not the players alone or the management. It was a culmination, and there was desperate need for a radical change if we were to salvage the season.

When the whistle blew, the boos were almost deafening. The players and management quickly made their way to the tunnel. I am sure that Les Reed must have felt very lonely walking along the touchline, but it was clear his time was up. Despite the anger and frustration, I had to feel a bit sorry for him. Reed is a Charlton man and understands the club and its fans. Maybe if he had been appointed in June ahead of Dowie, or even if he were not part of Dowie's regime, things would have been different. However, the reality was things were going disastrously, and Reed was not the man for the job. The fans wanted Pardew; but the board had not covered themselves in glory in the previous six months, so we did not know what to expect.

Unbelievably our chairman, Richard Murray, had said he would stand by Reed, another example of the board letting the fans down. Surely the Wycombe game told the board everything they needed to know about the situation we were in. At this stage it seemed as though there would be quite an atmosphere at our next home game, when surely the fans would again make their feelings clear.

Peter Varney, our chief executive, also came out in support of Reed and stated there would be money to spend in January. No matter who was in charge, there needed some investment in the team; the worry was, though, that by the time January came around, we'd be well and truly doomed to the Championship.

In Murray's support of Reed, Iain Dowie was also criticised for his transfer policy, Diawara singled out for costing so much money. This seemed a bit rich. The board had backed Dowie by giving him £11 million and sanctioned the signings. They were right to say the problems at the club started before Reed's appointment, but this did not change the fact the performances were embarrassing at times. Our squad needed change, but it was not that bad. We had players who had enough ability to play in the top flight, and Reed had to take a lot of the blame for our performances after Dowie left.

The final game before Christmas was away to Middlesbrough, which in previous years would have been seen as winnable. Judging by the last three games, there was little chance of us picking up a result. Reed went with a negative 5–4–1 formation; it failed, and we lost again, this time 2–0. Even though there were not many away fans at the Riverside that day, they made it clear that Reed had to go.

Even though the buck ultimately stops with the manager, the players under Reed let him down. Against Wycombe and Liverpool, there was no desire or commitment to do well. If the players had responded, the results would not have been so bad. The team had, if anything, gotten stronger since Reed took over. Andy Reid was getting fitter by the week, so there was no excuse saying that the team's putout was not full strength.

Even though we avoided the stigma of being bottom at Christmas, it did not change the fact that under Reed, survival looked impossible. Darren Bent – probably our most reliable player – had not scored since Dowie had left and was a shadow of the player who should have gone to a World Cup. When he failed to perform, there was not much hope as no one else would score the goals, especially with Reid injured. Under Dowie there were a lot of injuries and some bad luck thrown in as well. Les Reed had almost a full squad to pick from, and the games we lost were our own fault.

Going into the festive period, I thought it best to avoid thinking about football and Charlton too much. But then, late in the afternoon on Christmas Eve, news broke on Sky that Reed had left the club and Alan Pardew was our new manager. Suddenly I could not wait for more football and felt very positive. The next few fixtures, especially at home, looked winnable. Under Pardew, without even hearing his first conference, confidence had already been lifted.

Throughout the Premiership years, Charlton had been seen as a model for other clubs to follow, not only for teams trying to establish themselves in the top flight but also for teams with managerial problems. For many Charlton fans, the departure of Curbishley meant that for the first time we'd need a new manager, and now after only a few months, we had become like many other clubs with managerial turmoil. Over the years it had been taken for granted how lucky Charlton were to have a manager as good as Curbs was to stay for so long. Obviously he was linked with other posts on more than one occasion. Many times when Newcastle or Tottenham struggled to find the right man I saw these clubs and the goings on as farcical. Now it was at Charlton's turn to be the pantomime.

Reed's tenure was the shortest ever by a Premiership manager, and the League Managers Association rightly criticised the club for having three managers in such a short space of time. Their analysis that this was unacceptable was spot on. The board and players had to take a share of the blame. The fans had more than enough reason to feel short changed since May. After Curbs being at the helm for fifteen years, the turnover at the club was completely new for Charlton fans. Unlike after Curbs' and Dowie's departures there would be no speculation as to the successor.

It was unclear whether Reed was sacked or the decision was mutual for him to leave. With no newspaper on Christmas Day, the reports on Boxing Day would be very interesting. To leave a job so close to Christmas cannot have been pleasant for Les Reed, but now Alan Pardew was in charge, survival looked possible and we had the man we wanted to properly replace Curbishley.

Chapter 4

THE MESSIAH?

Our first game under Alan Pardew was at home to Fulham. Some might say this was one of the best fixtures Pardew could have hoped for. A home game under the floodlights against a side that rivalled ours for poor away form with 27,000 fans in good voice and fully behind the new manager, three points against Fulham seemed very possible. Survival was in no way going to be easy but felt more in our reach. After the last two disastrous appointments, 'Super Al' had the potential to be a long-term true successor to Alan Curbishley.

Pardew had played for Charlton under Curbs and had good management credentials, so he seemed a great choice. At Reading he had done an excellent job in getting them promotion and into the championship playoffs, and despite a sour end, had done well at West Ham. The West Ham job is one of the Premierships biggest, with tremendous pressure; and their fans are not always easy to please. Pardew did not have a great start, but after turmoil under Glenn Roeder, Pardew got them promoted. In their first season back, he not only stabilised the club but also got them within three minutes of winning the FA Cup. Not bad.

Things began to go wrong at West Ham when, not coincidentally there was a new owner, Eggert Magnusson, and the two Argentineans signed. It is hard to imagine these two players were brought in completely under Pardew's orders. When a manager is not allowed to manage alone, there are going to be problems. When Pardew was sacked from West Ham, he may have lost the dressing room, but the situation at West Ham was arguably easier to resurrect than ours was. West Ham still had an abundance of talent. Charlton needed some strengthening.

Because the appointment was on Christmas Eve meant that there was a wait for his first press release and the facts about Reed's departure. Even the Fulham programme had been published too late to include Pardew's appointment. Les Reed's match-day column was still there, from which one could tell how much Reed cared about the club as he talked of how he has pictures of our Wembley triumph on his wall. But Pardew was now the man in charge. Unlike his two predecessors, Pardew got a hugely favourable reception when he was introduced to the crowd. Chants of 'Super Al' rang around the Valley again.

Following Les Reed's departure, there were reports that he had allowed the players a Christmas party and given them Christmas Day off, this following the Wycombe loss. Apparently this was the final straw for the board as they realised he was too much of a soft touch and lacked the authority needed to be a top manager. However, only time would tell whether this decision was too late.

The Fulham game could have been a massive turning point in our season; if we had won, it could have really set us up for the remainder and given Pardew the prefect start. Fulham took the lead early on after some poor defending, but we hit back with two goals before half-time, Darren Bent finding his form at the right time to put us in front. Late on we were nervous, and understandably the defence dropped too deep. It looked as though we were going to hang on until, in the last minute of injury time, Fulham were awarded the most ridiculous free kick I have ever seen. This is no exaggeration.

Their attacker clearly handballed the ball so it went out of play. Unjustifiably the linesman awarded them a free kick, not a throw or a free kick to us, which would have been the correct decision. Typically Fulham equalized from the free kick. Even though the defending was again poor, the goal was a direct consequence of the decision. The boos at the end rivalled those of the Wycombe game, but this time they were for the referee and his assistants.

Graham Poll was the referee; he was not too far from the incident and would have surely seen what really happened. Poll is now retired, thankfully. He was a good referee at times, but the best refs are often those who you do not notice. Poll did all he could to get noticed. In some games it was almost the two teams and Graham Poll's ego. I say this not only because of the Fulham game as I am sure many fans and players feel the same about Poll. It felt that Poll thought he was some kind of celebrity and was more important than the players were. In his autobiography (why does a ref need an autobiography?) Poll wrote about the decision and made out that it was our fault for not defending the free kick properly.

The defending was admittedly not great, but this was the ninety-fourth minute of Charlton's most important game of the season. There were nerves, and the decision was not a difficult 50–50. There is no way Fulham should have got a free kick. Even writing this nearly two and a half years later, it hurts massively and angers me that this decision was costly.

Alan Pardew had had an instant impact. The performance was much better, and we clearly deserved to win. Darren Ambrose had a good chance to make it 3–1, which also hurts looking back, but the confidence had returned. Bent was back on goal trail, which was a massive boost. The only negative thoughts in my head – aside from those directed at the officials – were questions over time and whether the job was too big.

On the Saturday we played Aston Villa at home in one of the most enjoyable matches of the season. With Arsenal next up at the Emirates, this was a must win. Four points from the two home games would have been a decent return, even though on paper Fulham looked more winnable. In the Villa programme, the Reed situation was explained: Les Reed left by mutual consent and was thanked for his efforts. Not surprisingly there was no reference to the Christmas-party fiasco.

Luckily Villa were not in great form, and because of the previous performance, hopes were still high. In the match-day programme, Pardew had his first chance to address the fans. I thought he came across well, knowing what he was like at West Ham and Reading. It was evident he was a passionate manager who was determined to give the job 100 per cent. The thing that pleased me most about Pardew's appointment was that he was there for the long term. If we were ultimately relegated, he would have had half a season to get to know the players and would be the best man to mount a charge back.

After the Villa game, people believed that survival was possible. In the first half, ex-Palace keeper Kiraly made an outstanding save to deny Ambrose, but Villa led through a penalty. In the second half, we turned it around. First, Darren Bent scored again before Rommedahl had one of those moments we knew he was capable of but rarely produced. He ran half the length of the field and was one on one with Kiraly. Gareth Barry, however, brought him down and was sent off.

Even though obviously I would have preferred the goal, we had more than twenty minutes against ten men. Charlton kept knocking at the door and should have been ahead. The bar and post denied us as well as Ambrose looking as though he prodded the ball over the line, but the linesman said no goal. If we had not gone on to win, there would have been even more controversy about a linesman costing us a result.

In the ninetieth minute, Bryan Hughes won it for us with a stooping header. Only three days before there had been agony in the last minute, but not today. The Valley erupted as we had got our deserved victory. Words could not describe the feelings when the ball went in. Pardew was a hero, the players looked good enough again and we had a real fighting chance. This had not seemed possible ten or so days before after the Wycombe game. Only a shocking decision had cost us six points, which would have been amazing, but four points that I am sure we would not have got under Reed was a huge step in the right direction.

I phoned Conor after the game. I was not sure whether it was a coincidence, but the last two games he had stayed away, and we had played well. We agreed that the January transfer window would be massively important and the home game against Boro two weeks later would be vital. From the Villa game, Darren Bent had committed his future to the club, which was a huge boost. After his struggles under Reed, it was likely he may have looked for a move in January. But now Pardew was there we had a proven goal scorer, which gave us an advantage over some of the other sides at the bottom. Unfortunately Bent had picked up an injury against Villa, and it was unclear how serious it was. What was clear, fit or not, Darren could do with some help up front.

Football around the festive period is always fantastic. Games are on television most days, and there is always great entertainment. Not everyone agrees with such a heavy fixture list and the fact players spend much of their festive period training and travelling, but as a fan there is nothing better than going to a match on Boxing Day or sitting down to watch festive *Soccer Saturday* with a mince pie or two. These games are also a great chance to get bad results or performances out of teams' systems. After the heartbreak or Fulham, it was less than seventy-two hours before another game.

Another slight downer after the Villa game was Sheffield United beating Arsenal, which meant they remained seven points ahead. Many expected Arsenal to get the win, but a spirited performance left Charlton still a fair distance from the safety mark. Another reason this was disappointing was that we were to play Arsenal next. After their defeat, they would be more than keen to avoid a repeat, especially with Thierry Henry returning from injury just in time.

Trying to remain positive was helped by West Ham's serious dip in form following Curbs' promising start. They lost three on the bounce to leave them only two points ahead. The third defeat was an astonishing 6–0 reverse at Reading. After seeing the highlights, it became apparent, despite West Ham's talented players, they had serious problems as well, especially in defence. Wigan were another side failing to repeat their success of the first season. They had a bad Christmas period, which obviously helped us as there was another team in danger of being sucked into the relegation picture. If Charlton were not in the relegation picture, it would have been an exciting battle to watch; at least five sides could go down.

Following the thriller against Villa, it was only a few days before we were playing again, this time away at Arsenal. It was Charlton's first visit to the Emirates, and what a stadium! Highbury had tradition and character, but the new arena was something else. One great thing about the Emirates is that it is only a few minutes' walk from Highbury, unlike some of the other new stadiums which are miles from town and encompass cinemas and restaurants. Going into the game even with no Darren Bent, there was still some optimism that a point was possible. One sub-plot surrounding the game involved a spat between Pardew and Wenger after West Ham's late winner against Arsenal in November.

Arsene Wenger had taken offence at Pardew's celebration. Having seen the clip and with an element of bias, I do not understand Wenger's grievance. At the time Pardew was under immense pressure, and talk of his sacking was constantly talked about in the press. His cause for celebration was just. Fair enough if it was not a ninetieth-minute winner, but one rule in football that is much criticized is players being booked for removing shirts after scoring. This is not so different to Pard's behaviour after this goal. Pardew did not remove his shirt (thank God), but his celebration was more than you normally see from a manager. But Alan Pardew had done a little dance the season before in the FA Cup, and there were no complaints from Steve McLaren of Rafa Benitez.

I have never scored a goal in professional football. But if a player experiences anything like the kind of emotion a fan does after certain goals, then a removal of a shirt is, in my opinion, not worthy of punishment, nor is a player hurdling the advertising boards to celebrate with his fans. If I ever scored an important goal for Charlton, I would go mental. This is the same for most players, especially those who support the club. One of the best goals I have seen in my lifetime is the Ryan Giggs dribble and shot against Arsenal in the cup. What made it more memorable was the celebration. Can you imagine if he had then been booked after such a legendary goal in one of the most vital games of the season?

Going into the Arsenal game, I completely supported Pardew and hoped he would have the opportunity to show us a celebration again. This was not to be the case as Arsenal as they often do destroyed us with their phenomenal football. Even if Darren Bent had been fit, it would have made no difference. Despite conceding four goals, Carson had a very good game, thankfully; otherwise it could have been very embarrassing. One save from Henry was world class, plunging to his left denying the

French striker a trademark goal after he opened himself up to place the ball in the corner. Despite the lack of British players in Arsenals squad, there is no doubt they play fantastic football, and if you are not on receiving end, it is fantastic to watch.

The game had a major talking point, regarding Arsenal's first goal from a penalty. With Luke Young injured, our young right back, Osei Sankofa, had come in and applied himself well; however, he was sent off for denying a goal-scoring opportunity. Having seen it again, I think the decision to give a penalty looked dubious. Robin Van Persie, who was fouled, was clearly offside, and El Karkouri was also back there. Charlton's appeal highlights this. But to send a players off for such an offence, especially when a penalty is awarded, is a rule that needs to be altered.

A penalty and therefore probably a goal is punishment enough. The rule to send off goalkeepers for this is criticised and rightly so. In this game it effectively ended the game as a contest. Arsenal would have more than likely still gone on to win comfortably, but the fact Charlton went down to ten meant there was almost no chance of a comeback. The arguments against a change include the view that a goalkeeper could save the penalty, and if the foul was deliberate, the offender has effectively avoided punishment. This is true, but a solution would be to give the refs more discretion as to whether they believe it is deliberate. Therefore, if a player genuinely goes for the ball, a penalty alone should be given. If a deliberate denial of a goal scoring opportunity occurs, a red card does seem more justified.

Arsenal scored two goals late on to add gloss to the result. We could have no complaints about Arsenal completely outplaying us. Getting anything from Arsenal would have been a bonus. We knew that there were far more important games ahead. Due to results over Christmas, the next set of Premiership fixtures took on extra significance. Charlton were at home to Middlesbrough, who themselves were not out of danger, whilst West Ham were playing Fulham, who had one of the worst away records in the league.

Before these games, there was the third round of the FA Cup. Charlton played at Nottingham Forest and were embarrassingly beaten 2–0. Despite fielding a strong team, Charlton just were not good enough on the day. Not that anyone was too despondent as the league was far more important, and with Darren Bent injured, we could ill afford any more absentees.

The following week Alan Pardew did his first bit of business in the window. Although we had already secured the Chinese captain – Zheng Zhi – on loan till the end of the season, there was no guarantee he would be a success. There was obviously a major difference between the Chinese leagues and the Premiership despite Zheng himself saying he was China's best player. Pardew's signing was Ben Thatcher from City. Despite his disciplinary problems, he was a steady, experienced left back who had played in relegation battles before. The only worry was that he was known for the odd lapse of discipline. But for £500,000 he would prove to be more reliable than Traore was, who was sold to Portsmouth for £1 million. In just over six months, we had made £1 million pounds loss of

Traore, but we were just pleased he had left; Portsmouth now had the misfortune to have him.

When Les Reed was in charge, we were linked with the Hibernian pair Scott Brown and Kris Thompson. Although they were highly rated, there is a big difference between the Scottish Premiership and the English Premiership. Four million pounds seemed a lot of money. Charlie Nicholas said on Sky he did not think that they were ready for the step up, so it was no loss when Hibs rejected the bid. Ironically the pair have gone to establish themselves for the two Old Firm clubs and look like being Scotland regulars for years to come, so in hindsight their signings would have been excellent business.

Before the Middlesbrough game, the FA decided to increase Sankofa's ban to two games after they deemed our appeal against his red card 'frivolous'. Charlton argued that Sankofa was not the last man; and Van Persie was offside. Of course I agreed, and with replays so should have the FA. With Luke Young injured, it was a massive blow to lose Sankofa for another game. On the plus side, we had Andy Reid back from injury.

The Boro game felt massive. If we won, and results went our way, we would be just three points from seventeenth and in touching distance of a host of other teams. Despite not having Darren Bent, many believed we could get a result. Boro had not won away all season, to give us further hopefulness. Ultimately Boro turned out probably their best away performance of the season, despite Hasselbaink doubling his league goal tally for the season.

Boro hit back with three goals, the killer second a real howler at the back from Hreidarsson. Results elsewhere went out way, but with some tricky games coming up, this game felt like a massive kick in the balls. The game would be the last we would see of Andy Reid for the season. In his only appearance under Pardew, the injury jinx hit us again, and he'd be a massive loss.

When you lose the proverbial six-pointer, it is hard to take. What was still clear was the lack of firepower up front. There was still no one who would regularly score the goals with Darren out for the next few games. This needed to be addressed in the window. West Ham broke the bank to bring in some reinforcements. They spent big on Matt Upson, Davenport, Lucas Neill and Nigel Quashie. Signing Quashie seemed strange as he had been relegated from the Premiership with almost every club he had been at. For a Charlton fan, this was great news as there was even more reason to believe West Ham would probably go down.

Other teams also strengthened their attack. Wigan brought in Caleb Folan, who had done very well in League One and in the cup competitions (including a goal against Charlton). Sheffield United signed Jon Stead, who, despite not being prolific, had scored goals to save Blackburn three years previously and had done well in the Championship. Halfway through the window it felt as though we needed to follow suit and bring someone in. Even a loan signing or a bargain from the lower leagues would have surely made a difference and given us a boost.

Charlton were heavily linked with Anthony Stokes from Arsenal. He had been on loan at Falkirk in the Scottish Premier League and scored a lot of goals, including against the Old Firm. As a young player with bags of potential, he seemed an exciting signing. Two million pounds was a lot of money if we failed to stay up, but the standard of the SPL is still fairly high, so sixteen in eighteen is remarkable. However, he chose to go to Championship side Sunderland partly because of their manager, Roy Keane. This was a blow to lose out to a lower division side, yet there was the chance they would replace us in the top flight.

Stokes has not proved to be such a big hit in England, nevertheless he is still young so has plenty of time to make a mark. After losing out on Stokes, we still should have looked at other striking options. There were strikers in the Championship who could handle the step up and would not cost too much. It felt like an opportunity lost that we did not try to strengthen the front line.

After being very downbeat following the Boro game, we had two very difficult away games at Portsmouth and Bolton; these would then be followed by home and away games against Chelsea and Manchester United, respectively. On paper it looked as though any sort of return from these games would be a bonus, especially as all four teams were either in or near to the top six.

First up, away at Pompey. Amazingly we won our first away game since October 2005, which was also at Fratton Park. In 2005 we were near to the top of the league, and Portsmouth were struggling. Here the roles were completely reversed. We could take inspiration from Portsmouth as at Christmas 2005 they brought in their messiah, Harry Redknapp, after a difficult start. A win against City as late as March proved to be the catalyst for an amazing run which saved them from what seemed like certain relegation.

During their run in early 2006, I saw Portsmouth play at Upton Park when they destroyed Alan Pardew's West Ham 4–2. You could see that Harry had Pompey playing with great confidence and belief; of course they had talented players, including Pedro Mendes, who scored a worldly. This season they had carried on and looked on course for Europe, with some astute signings, such as Sol Campbell and Kanu. Looking at Pompey's model gave Charlton great cause for optimism.

The game at Fratton Park in January 2007 was a typical smash-and-grab raid from the away side. We scored late through an Amady Faye fluky deflected effort, the kind of goal that normally goes against you when you are near the bottom. The last few minutes was nerve wracking. Only a class save from Carson preserved the three points, but this win was such a boost. Tony Adams, Portsmouth's assistant, said we came into the game with the look of a team expecting to get beat. To be fair this was perhaps true, but a huge amount of credit must go the players for taking advantage of Portsmouth not being at the races.

Ben Thatcher, public enemy number one, at Fratton Park turned in a solid and disciplined performance, to his credit after a lengthy early season ban following the Mendes incident. Marcus Bent played up front on his own, led the line terrifically and worked his socks off. The only thing lacking was a goal.

The win away at Pompey was made even better by the fact West Ham and Sheffield United failed to win. This was the time in the season when other results were really beginning to matter. Psychologically to see our rivals drop points can sometimes help make up for your own defeat or as was the case here make your win seem more than just three points.

A credible draw away at Bolton followed. The Pardew spirit showed through as after conceding early we fought back to get the draw. Although again Bolton may not have been at their best, we exploited this and deserved to return home with something. Luck was starting to follow us as well after sneaking a win against Pompey. The equaliser was a goalkeeping error from the normally dependable Bolton keeper.

Conor and I discussed going to Bolton. However, two seasons before he had been to our first two away games at Bolton and Man City, and we lost by four on both occasions. With his win record at games this season standing at one, coupled with my away win ratio, there was no way we were going to jeopardise Charlton's chances.

After the defeat to Boro, and with the forthcoming fixtures, we felt doomed. But four points from two teams with impressive home records was superb. Our record at the Reebok Stadium especially was quite poor (two 4–1 defeats in 2004 and 2006) so to get a point really raised spirits.

West Ham were still struggling and the following night lost at home to Liverpool to keep them down near the foot. Whilst other teams above were not too far away, Sheffield United remained seven points ahead. We still had to play both teams at the Valley, and there was a long way to go.

Prior to the Chelsea home game, we bought in two more players. Alex Song came on loan from Arsenal, and Madjid Bougherra signed from Sheffield Wednesday for £2 million. Despite the lack of strikers, these two looked excellent buys. Song was very highly rated at Arsenal and would add some tenacity and class to our midfield. I have talked about the lack of a creative spark in there, and even though Song was not to be the answer, he had a good range of passing and energy. Bougherra was a snip at £2 million; he had done very well for Wednesday and represented good business as even if we were relegated, he had proved to be one of the Championship's best.

Unfortunately like Zheng, both new players were not available for Chelsea but would play a significant role. At home to Chelsea, we fell behind early to a Lampard goal, and most expected a comfortable away win. However, we bounced back well and should have got a point. Despite Carson showing again why he should be an England candidate, we had the better chances. Unluckily they both fell to Faye, who showed why his goal against Pompey was only his first in English football. Petr Cech did his bit in the Faye chances. But you can't help but feel if they had fallen to anyone else, we'd have had a valuable point.

Alan Pardew had said that if we had Darren Bent fit for the Boro game, we'd probably have won. Against Chelsea I am sure we would have at least got a goal. Marcus Bent had done well on his own up front but was not a goal threat and possibly would be better deployed on the right of midfield. Kevin Lisbie had come back from injury and was capable of a goal but had not scored for a very long time; and of course when working your way back from long term injuries, it takes time to get your best form back.

Against Chelsea we created enough to score at least. This was the type of game, in my view, that if we'd kept hold of someone like Johansson, he'd have found a finish when it mattered. J.J., as he was known, struggled to score goals regularly but was a fine finisher with both feet, and it was a mistake not trying to keep him at the club. His trademark overhead kicks were legendary as they saved some valuable points in his early years at the club.

One interesting aspect of the Chelsea game was Shevchenko's play. Chelsea had smashed their transfer record for the Ukrainian who was regarded as one of the world's best. However, in England he had looked a shadow of his former self, and at the Valley he looked off the pace and was no threat even to our dodgy back line. Not that I would have rejected him if he appeared in our front line as he would have beefed up our attack. There were rumours his signing was not completely Jose Mourinho's. This is yet another example of when chairman's intervention goes too far and undermines a manager leading to conflict.

With Charlton's dismal away form and poor record at Old Trafford, going into the United away game, anything other than a home win would have been a massive bonus I have been lucky enough to go to Old Trafford and it is a fantastic stadium with a cracking atmosphere despite criticism about the prawn sandwich brigade. This Saturday though I was at home with *Soccer Saturday*. The Charlton game was not the only game I was interested in. Sheffield United were at home to Spurs, and West Ham had a vital home game with bottom side Watford.

Charlton fell short at Old Trafford, but it took to the last ten minutes for United to finish us off. Charlton played well, had a few openings and may have deserved a point. Another major plus was the three debutants – Bougherra, Song and Zheng – impressing and showing some quality. Nevertheless, a 2–0 reverse at Old Trafford is not too bad, and with West Ham losing at home to Watford, Charlton were the team playing better and seemingly with more of a chance of survival.

It was possible that both teams would be relegated, especially as Sheffield United beat Spurs to ensure they were ten points above the drop zone. Even with a lot of points to play for, ten points is a very healthy lead, and on 10 February Sheffield United looked almost safe. For Charlton, though, the next two matches were amongst the biggest in our recent history (excluding Wembley 1998), away at Watford but first at home to Alan Curbishley's West Ham.

Chapter 5

NOW WE REALLY BELIEVE

The Charlton and West Ham scenario was astonishing. Going into the game on 24 February 2007, both teams were locked on twenty points. Each manager had very strong links with the other side. Curbishley was a Charlton legend, with 749 games in charge and someone who forever would be welcomed back to the club. At West Ham he had struggled to make an impact, and his job was under serious threat. Pardew, on the other hand, had fallen out of love with the Hammers and was now being hailed as a potential Charlton hero.

The two weeks between the Manchester United and West Ham games seemed to take an age. The match really felt like a cup final as there was so much on it. I don't think I have ever been as nervous before a Charlton game as this one. It was billed as a game which neither side could afford to lose. Normally a two-week break from football in mid season is welcome as it provides a welcome rest from the worry. But the fact we had two clear weeks between the United away game and West Ham meant there was even more time to worry.

Charlton had their two England internationals (Luke Young and Darren Bent) back from injury, and we were the side in better form, albeit not necessarily in terms of results. West Ham had players who had played for Charlton; Paul Konchesky, for example, had spent many years at the Valley and had left only to pursue first-team football. However, the focus was understandably on the management. Curbishley would of course receive a warm welcome back. When he left the club in 2006, he said it was unique for a manager to leave a club in such circumstances, with his head held high and with so much support. When Sir Alex Ferguson leaves United, I am sure the circumstances will be similar, although the chances of their being involved in relegation the season after are somewhat slimmer.

No one could have predicted the half-time score: Charlton were leading 3–0 and deservedly so. We had destroyed West Ham, whose defence fell apart every time we attacked. Jerome Thomas had one of his best performances and scored a fine individual goal, and Darren Bent returned with a well-taken goal. Darren Ambrose was superb for us in midfield, scoring one and assisting Thomas to help us deal with the loss of Reid.

The West Ham fans turned on their manager. Chants rang out of the away end along the lines of 'We want Alan Pardew back' and 'You don't know what you're doing'. To see Alan Curbishley go through this was not pleasant, despite the obvious delight at our own performance. I have never seen fans turn on their manager and team so much. Of course West Ham had talented players and their performance was terrible, but similarly to the Les Reed situation against Wycombe, it is difficult not to feel for the manager getting the abuse.

The atmosphere coming from the home fans was excellent. Alan Pardew was the most popular man at the ground. Even West Ham fans ironically joined in with our chants of 'Super Al'. We really believed that Charlton could stay up. There was now a manager capable of succeeding Curbs, and with a drastic improvement in the playing staff, Charlton looked like it was getting back to the days of Curbs.

At half-time, as a pessimist I still thought the game was not over; 3–0 is a lead rarely turned around, but it does happen, and with an early reply there is always a chance. When we were three goals up at Arsenal in 2001, apparently after we missed a chance of a fifth, Curbs commented that we may rue the miss. When Hasselbaink hit a post a couple of minutes after the break, the same thought went through my head.

After about fifty minutes, Carlos Tevez had a free kick from just outside the box, which Carson made another good stop on. If that had gone in, there'd have been 40 minutes with a nervous Charlton defending a two-goal lead, which is always precarious.

As it turned out, we defended quite well and looked more likely to score again. Jerome Thomas scored his second with another fine finish, by which time most of the West Ham fans in the away end had left. Four to nil was by far our best result of the season. There were some great individual performances –Thomas was superb out wide – but my man of the match was Alex Song. He stood out in the centre of midfield with his fine range of passing and tenacity, oozing Arsenal class.

One player on the West Ham side that you had to feel sympathy for was their goalkeeper, Rob Green. He had played in the 6–0 defeat at Reading and now was playing in this heavy defeat. Green is a class goalkeeper, and when looking at the goals it is hard to attribute blame to him. Clearly the defence in front of him were turning in abysmal performances. Even in such a game, Green still made some good saves and was probably West Ham's best player. In the summer there were reports we were going to sign Green from Norwich, but he opted to go to West Ham, which was no bad thing as we got Carson. Both, in my opinion, are excellent England-class keepers.

English goalkeepers have faced criticism in recent years for not being good enough. This particular season all the potential England number ones excelled, despite a couple being in struggling sides. Carson was by far our player of the year. David James and Ben Foster also had superb seasons. I never saw the likes of Shilton, Clemence or Banks play, but having seen the modern-day English keepers I see there is great quality there.

Ben Foster was injured for our away game at Watford. This was a boost as he had preserved a point for them at the Valley, so there was even more optimism when – as usual – I turned to *Soccer Saturday*. West Ham were not playing until the next day, so the focus was with our game. On paper we were expected to win, Watford faced a huge uphill task if they were to survive. In all honesty the season before, when they came up through the playoffs, promotion was perhaps a season too soon.

After the week before, the first half against Watford was a little bit like after the Lord Mayor's Show as we fell two behind. Apparently Charlton were not playing badly, just struggling at the back. But in the second half, we fought back with two late goals to salvage a 2–2. With ten minutes to go, everyone associated with Charlton would have taken a point, but after equalizing in the last minute, we had a fantastic chance to win it. Lisbie went through one on one but fluffed his lines. Suddenly a draw felt like a huge disappointment, and we were rueing two points dropped.

However, our form was good. When assessing the season to that point, the one major question surrounded where we would be had Pardew been in charge earlier or the board had not let the fans down with Les Reed's appointment. It seemed that with the squad we now had, a mid table finish would have been a certainty. Safety was nowhere near assured, but with a decent run of home games and fixtures against the teams above, it was in our own hands.

The next day West Ham were involved in one of the best games of the season. Carlos Tevez scored his first goal in English football, a fine free kick, but Tottenham went on the win the game 4–3, the final goal deep into injury time. West ham deserved something from the game, but they had no luck, and even one of their biggest fans, ex-striker Tony Cottee, admitted it looked like they'd be playing Championship football next season. Again Curbs looked a lonely figure on the touchline. When the winning goal went in, you could see the anger on his face. This was clearly hurting him just as much as it hurt most West Ham fans.

West Ham won against Blackburn the week later. This match was overshadowed by the winning goal, which was up there with the Fulham decision for the craziest of the season. Carlos Tevez was on the goal line in an offside position when the ball from Zamora's shot hit him and rebounded. Inexplicably the linesman awarded a goal when the ball was not even close to crossing the line. If Tevez were a defender, it would have been praised as a good goal line clearance. This again opened up the debate about goal line and video technology.

I see no reason why video technology should not be introduced into football, not for any decision but to start those around whether the ball has crossed the line. To have another official or even to delegate to the fourth official assessing whether the ball has gone in would be quick and effective. The fourth official is always a trained referee. It would take him a matter of seconds to look at the incident on a monitor and tell the referee the correct decision. Goal line decisions are the most important a referee and a linesman have to make, so there is a need for further assistance. If there is a situation similar to the one in the Champions League semi-final between Liverpool and Chelsea when, nearly four years after the event, no one knows if the ball crossed the line despite thousands of TV replays, then there should be no goal.

The famous Pedro Mendes effort for Spurs, also in 2005, was miles in and would have taken a second to resolve. Likewise with the Zamora 'goal' this season. People argue that this would slow the game down, but this would not be the case if there were a monitor or a screen the fourth or maybe even fifth official could access straight away. The delay would not even be as long as those when a substitution is being made. In tennis it adds to the excitement (I am writing in summer, Wimbledon is on) when the video shows whether the ball is in or out. Certainly in football it would add tension to the proceedings and ensure less criticism of the officials.

The first of our vital home games was against the inconsistent Newcastle on Mother's Day. Fortunately my mum had a season ticket, so there was no conflict over the match and a family dinner. This would have caused an argument otherwise as this was another huge game for Charlton and one I would no way have missed. Newcastle had been knocked out of the UEFA Cup the previous Thursday and had injury problems at the back, so Charlton had a slight advantage.

After an even first half, Martins missed a glorious chance for Newcastle, and a matter of moments later we scored. Zheng Zhi scored his first goal for the club following up a free kick from Darren Bent which hit the bar. We played the better football in the second half and got the second through a stonewall penalty which Jerome Thomas dispatched; 2–0 was a fine result, and the safety margin was now well within reach. We were four points behind Sheffield United with them still to come to the Valley and Wigan who were not too far ahead up next.

One thing that Pardew brought to the club was opera singers before the game. He thought this would help improve the atmosphere and inspire the fans and players. To be honest, if this were at another club, I would have thought it sounded a bit bullshitty, but as Pardew had transformed the club and was doing well, there seemed no reason to question this. Anything to ensure the atmosphere at the ground would be top draw could only be a good thing for us; the atmosphere at the Valley was probably the best I had ever heard in the last few weeks of this season.

Next up, another six-pointer against Wigan. This was no classic. Neither keeper was tested, much but with five minutes to go, we got a penalty. This had the potential to be the most important kick of Darren Bents career as he stepped up. He showed tremendous nerve, and we had a priceless three points which dragged Wigan right into the mix. We were one point from safety as the Charlton Web site stated survival once a dream was now really on. Even though a draw would have been a fair result, we had momentum. It was a case of 'bring on the next match'.

As Wigan protested there was a small wait for the penalty. Even though 27,000 fans were willing the ball in, this was the most important penalty a Charlton player had taken since the '98 playoff final. Sometimes when there is wait for a penalty the opposition can psych out the taker. If any Wigan players tried to play mind games with Bent, they didn't work.

As at Christmas the Easter fixtures come thick and fast, and have a major say in your team's fate. Numerous teams have ensured survival over the Easter weekend, and even though we could not ensure survival, a healthy return would go a long way. On the other side, with some poor results we'd be almost down.

On Good Friday we played away at Man City, the day before everyone else was due to play, which gave us the chance to climb out of the bottom three for the first time since September. Another game that was not a classic ended in a 0–0, which looked a good result considering we had won once away all season. However, as in the Watford game, we rued what might have been as Zheng had a one on one with ten minutes to go, which went wide. Despite the psychological boost a draw gave us as – we were out of the bottom three – a win would have been superb, but it was another clean sheet and solid performance.

This meant the next day I could sit at home, watch *Soccer Saturday* and hope results elsewhere went our way. Wigan and Sheffield United both lost home games, which were massive boosts, especially as they would have been predicted to win against Bolton and Newcastle, respectively. However, West Ham, who were coming back into the mix, won again, surprisingly at Arsenal. We were still seventeenth, and West Ham looked amazingly like they could stay up. At Arsenal they scored a goal on the break and relied on Rob Green to turn in a superb performance. Survival was still a big ask for the Hammers as they had some difficult games – but stranger things have happened.

Two days later, on Easter Monday, we played after everyone else in a night game against Reading at home. For the third game on the trot, the game was nothing special; another 0–0 was not the end of the world. Neither keeper was severely tested, but we did hit the bar early on through Karkouri. If that had gone in, who knows? Instead we had to settle for a point.

Graham Poll was back at the Valley and yet again involved in controversy, this time in favour of us. Alex Song, who was on a yellow card, made a challenge that normally would have resulted in another one. He was let off, and Poll signalled to our bench. This was soon followed by Song's substitution, which caused questions over Poll from both pundits and Reading. If this happened to another side, we would feel hard done by, but following Poll's role in the Fulham game, things had almost evened themselves out.

I felt very disappointed after the Reading game as they had left out their top goal scorer in Kevin Doyle, and three points were ours for the taking. The performance had been solid but not adventurous enough. If we had thrown extra men forward and gambled, their defence may have faltered. Also, if we had beaten Reading, there would have been a big gap between us and Sheffield United. After a draw there was the possibility we would need to win an away game as well as the home games, which would be a big ask.

The following weekend we played away at Everton on the Sunday. The day before Sheffield United had played West Ham at Bramall Lane in a game where a draw would have been the perfect result. In the end the home side won 3–0, and we were back in the bottom three. But going into the Everton game, despite Everton near the top end of the table, there was real hope we could maintain our good form. And we played well, but after equalizing late through Darren Bent and seemingly grabbing a priceless point, James McFadden won the game for the hosts with one of the goals of the season. As against Fulham at home, we were heartbroken. Charlton had enough chances to win the game but ended up feeling sick. Our unbeaten run was over, and now the home game with Sheffield United was very important.

After the West Ham game nearly two months previously, I did not think I would feel so nervous before a game, but this seemed more significant. After being ten points ahead of eighteenth in February, Sheffield United had been inconsistent, and their away form was patchy. With our recent home results, we had to be confident of a result.

The club placed clappers on the seats to improve the atmosphere. This worked as the home fans were by far the louder. But neither side could break through in the first half. In the second a spectacular effort from Talal El Karkouri (Elk) from a mile out put us in the lead. Some guy behind where I was sitting commented that it would now certainly be a draw. There was a long way to go, but nerves immediately set in, and not long after Sheffield United equalized through Stead, a well taken goal but a massive blow to silence the home crowd.

In the last twenty minutes we pressed hard for a winner but could not break through. United did not threaten to win the game, but they defended well. We did not test their keeper enough and could not make our dominant possession count.

At the end it was the away fans singing 'We are staying up', and it was hard to disagree. Sheffield United's fixtures look winnable, whereas we had to go to Blackburn and Liverpool and play a home game against Tottenham.

The walk up the hill after the game was very depressing; you could sense the despondency amongst other Charlton fans. We felt we had blown it. Even though it was extraordinary considering where we were when Pardew took over, with three games to go it was still all to play for. A win against Sheffield United would have been huge, especially considering West Ham's good run was continuing and Sheffield United had it in their own hands.

In 2005–6 Charlton had launched Operation Riverside for their FA Cup quarter-final at Boro This included free coach travel to ensure the best away following, and it worked despite a disappointing result. For our next game away at Blackburn, Charlton launched Operation Ewood. We took nearly 6,000 fans to the game. By all accounts our fans were superb; unfortunately the team were not.

Scott Carson rightly won our player of the year award in the week before Blackburn, but unluckily he made a howler in the game to put them in front. Having watched the season's goals over again, I think this was probably the only goal of the whole season where blame could be attributed to Carson. On one or two goals, if you were being over critical, you could say Scott could have done better. But he had earned numerous points for us. Without him we would have been dead and buried.

Ben Thatcher also did not have his finest moment as he was sent off for two yellows, the second being a rash challenge, which in the circumstances seemed very stupid. He had proved his doubters right, which was a shame, as he had fitted in well since signing. However, Darren Bent (who else again?) gave us hope with an equalizer as the travelling contingent went mental. We could not hold out and even though a 4–1 reverse was harsh, it was a massive uphill task.

Part of me was gutted. I was not there with the 5,000 fans. Having not been to enough away games anyway, I felt disloyal. Then again to have gone all that way and seen our Premier League hopes fade away would have been horrible. It was bad enough watching *Soccer Saturday*, especially as results did not go our way.

Charlton heavily missed Diawara in this game as in recent weeks he had really shown his class. It was no coincidence that at Watford and now Blackburn he had been missing and our old bad ways had returned. Maybe when Richard Murray said of Diawara when he signed that he 'was the best defender you had never heard of' he was spot on, despite the gloves.

West Ham went and thrashed Wigan at the JJB. Carlos Tevez scored again, which meant both sides still could go either way. Fulham were also in the mix after a poor run, meaning Chris Coleman had been lost his job despite doing an excellent job in his four years in charge. Coleman's replacement was Lawrie Sanchez, who brought in Les Reed as well to add a further twist. Therefore going into the last two games, Watford were relegated, but it was two teams from Charlton, West Ham, Wigan, Sheffield United and Fulham for the neutral one of the most interesting relegation battles for years.

Charlton's penultimate game was at home to Spurs on a Monday night; this meant everyone played before us on the Saturday. As I sat down to watch *Soccer Saturday*, Charlton desperately needed results to go our way, especially West Ham's home game with Bolton and Fulham hosting Liverpool. West Ham dispatched Bolton, so we had to rely on Liverpool doing us a favour; otherwise we would need six points from two games to even have a chance of staying up.

Liverpool had a Champion League's final to focus on so fielded a weakened side at Fulham. It showed as Fulham won to ensure their safety. On paper it looked as though their decision to sack Coleman was justified as they survived with one to play. Neil Warnock, not one to stay silent, was heavily critical of Liverpool not fielding their big guns. But as a Charlton fan, I found it difficult to find grievance as we were sure to play at Anfield the following week and would hope they'd do the same. Also after thirty-eight games, if you go down, you go down because of your own performances and results, not because of another team's weakened line-up in one game.

Our game being on the Monday proved to be a disadvantage as we now knew we had to win both games, whereas if we had played on the Saturday, we would have avoided this extra pressure. Going into the weekend fixtures, four points could have been enough, and with Liverpool's other commitments, Anfield did not seem the worst away trip.

There was now the real possibility that we would be relegated at the Valley on Sky. Conor had not been to many of Pardew's games except the defeats, and he was coming to the Spurs game. This was the writing on the wall as he was clearly a jinx. In some ways it felt fitting that he would be there for the final nail in the coffin.

Before the game we had an opera singer who had played twice before at the Valley. Both times we had won, so maybe this was a good omen. However, Spurs were a bit too good for us. Berbatov oozed class with the first goal, turning Elk as if he wasn't there before slotting past Carson. As we tried to press for an equalizer, Spurs contained us well, and there was no way through.

To add insult to injury, Jermaine Defoe scored the second to end our Premiership stay. Defoe had been with the club when he was younger and had left to go to West Ham in controversial circumstances, which ensured he always got a hostile reception at the Valley. Even though we had done well financially from Defoe as we got a share of his transfer from West Ham to Spurs as well as compensation for his departure, it was still a kick in the teeth for him to kill us off. Nevertheless, Defoe did not relegate us; the first half of the season did. If Pardew had come in earlier, I have no doubt we'd have had a successful season, but we were down and it hurt.

The Sky cameras were at the Valley, and no doubt the cameraman was on the lookout for any crying home fans. On my part there were no tears. It hurt, but in some ways I was more angry than disappointed. I was angry and bitter at our relegation as typically there were thousands of 'what-ifs', mainly surrounding the management and board but also if certain games had turned out differently. Fulham and Sheffield United are obvious examples, but late goals against us at Everton and Sheffield United are also painful memories.

On the final weekend of the season, it was one from West Ham, Wigan and Sheffield United The equation was simple: Wigan had to win otherwise they were down. If Wigan won, Sheffield United had to hope West Ham lost at Old Trafford for them to survive. West Ham needed a point from United, who themselves fielded a slightly understrength side with a cup final also in mind.

Charlton played at Anfield, which was now relatively insignificant except that it would be Robbie Fowler's last home game for Liverpool. Fowler had returned to Liverpool the season before and was an Anfield legend, possibly England's most natural goal scorer. If it weren't for some nasty injuries, surely he would have been an England regular and could have made a real difference at a major tournament. Going into the game, I thought he was bound to score.

We kept Fowler quiet, and Charlton turned in a fine performance to earn a draw. Liverpool scored in the last minute through a penalty by which time Fowler had left the action. Bent had scored again. (It seemed as though he would leave in the summer.) But there were reasons to look forward to the Championship. Darren Randolph had played well in goal in place of ineligible Carson whilst Bougherra and Lloyd Sam looked as though they would be effective in the second tier.

Wigan won at Sheffield United to ensure their survival with an outstanding performance. But it was at Old Trafford where events were most astonishing as West Ham won to send Sheffield United down. Rob Green was superb in goal. I must admit I was pleased to see Curbs keep West Ham up, not just because Curbs is such a legend, but you have to give him tremendous credit for keeping them up, especially considering where they were in early March. There was also the fact that West Ham would probably have walked the Championship if they had gone down. Thinking ahead to the next season, I felt as though Wigan and Sheffield United would be a similar level to us when trying to bounce back, so seeing West Ham survive was no bad thing.

Sheffield United have since been involved with both football and legal battles with West Ham over Carlos Tevez and whether he was properly registered and eligible to play. The Premier League fined West Ham more than £5 million for the signings of Tevez and Mascherano, but Sheffield United argued they should have had a points deduction therefore relegating West Ham. The Premier League refused to deduct points. Instead Sheffield United stayed involved in legal proceedings until March 2009. There has been a settlement, and West Ham reportedly had to pay United £20 million, payable over four years.

Tevez may not have been eligible, but he played a huge role in their survival. Seven goals in ten games as well as the winner at Old Trafford shows he was instrumental. Sheffield United went down not because of Tevez but because they were the third-worst team and Charlton were the second worse team. Over thirty-eight games no team is good enough to go down, and they end up where they deserve. Sheffield United can realistically have few complaints. Their points tally was not good enough. Sheffield United blew it as they were in February ten points clear.

Charlton also fully deserved to go down. At the time it felt as though we were hard done by; but despite poor decisions at times, we deserved relegation, especially looking at the pre-Pardew era. Dowie was unlucky as he had only twelve league games and more injury problems than you can usually expect. Nevertheless, his signings struggled generally, and he has to take a share of the blame. Traore and Faye sum up his signings as Traore was useless and Faye was not what we needed in midfield. The Les Reed era was one of Charlton's lowest. The board let the fans down by going with the cheap, easy option of Reed. The games he was in charge may as well have been written off. It was clear despite Reed being a nice guy and a Charlton man, he did not have the support of the players or fans, and we were going nowhere but down.

It was not until Alan Pardew came in that things began to change. Pardew did all he could to save us, and the performances under him were so much better. The critics may say he had enough games to save us and we blew it in the last few games, but he gave us a real fighting chance and no blame should go towards Pardew. His signings were top drawer and gave the club fresh impetus and belief; the team looked more than good enough to compete in the Premiership and gave the fans a real boost.

Relegation was made worse by the fact we would lose more than if we had gone a year or two before. there was not only the extra revenue, reports of a loss of £30 million as well as the certain departures of our three England Internationals. If we had survived, the chances are we could have afforded to reward Young and Bent with new contracts and buy Carson with the promise of regular Premier League football, as well as having the money to strengthen the squad and really challenge for the top ten maybe even higher.

If Darren Bent had not missed two months injured and then played games when perhaps he was not 100 per cent, who knows what might have happened? Andy Reid as well probably did not play a single game when he was fully fit. Pardew could have been the messiah. West Ham deservedly survived but it has to be said that they had Argentinean internationals and spent massively in the window. If we had had this luxury, we would have headed to Europe, not Scunthorpe.

Despite relegation many felt we could bounce back. Obviously players would leave, but with Pardew in charge, his promotion experience would be highly valuable. Judging by the fans' reactions, he had full support, and I had no doubt Pardew was the right man to lead our promotion charge as we attempted to bounce back at the first attempt. In 1999 after relegation we stormed the old First Division. First though it would be a busy summer.

Chapter 6

NEW FACES, NEW START

The summer of 2007 was one of the busiest in Charlton's history. Normally during the close season, the Web site has newsworthy reports only on a few days. Close season is always boring. Even if there is a tournament, there will still be Saturdays with nothing significant to do. Luckily Sky Sports has twenty-four-hour updates for transfer news, and there are usually seasonal highlights from the Premiership years on TV, so it is not all bad. This summer though it seemed as though it was nonstop as there was the highest turnover in players ever at Charlton.

Of course even the most optimistic Charlton fan knew that we would lose one or two players who we'd be sad to see leave, but there would also be players leaving who would not at all be missed. When teams are relegated from the Premiership, they get parachute payments which help them deal with the financial implications. This would mean there would be money to spend for players and – one would hope – build a side good enough to mount a promotion campaign.

Even though relegation was horrible, the prospect of a promotion was exciting. For the first time since 2000, we would be favourites in most matches. Most pundits predicted that we'd bounce back, and judging by the squad that was in place, so did the fans. A lot of non-Charlton fans commented along the lines of 'At least you'll win a few next year'; we hoped this would be the case.

Before the season starts, the chances are your club will be linked with numerous players. Most of these rumours will never have any weight; however, watching Sky Sports and reading the sports sections can still be very interesting. The problem with being a fan of more of a selling club is that you hate reading about teams wanting your players. In 2004 and 2006 during the transfer windows, we were involved in transfer sagas regarding Scott Parker and Danny Murphy. Every day it seemed as though there would be further developments, but hope of keeping them kept on fading. This year the most publicity would surely surround Darren Bent.

When predicting what type of players Pardew would go for, I expected he might follow a similar system to when he was at West Ham and got them promoted. In his promotion year, the side had a good blend of youth and experience. Players such as Reo Coker and Marlon Harewood were young and hungry. Reo Coker had done very well for Wimbledon and looked capable of playing in the Premiership. Harewood had scored a lot of goals for Forest and again looked as though he could do a job in the Premiership. Pardew also brought in players like Teddy Sheringham and our own Chris Powell to add much valued experience to the squad.

One slight worry about Pardew's policies at West Ham was that he signed a lot of players, some of which were not really good enough for a club like West Ham. With the greatest respect to players such as Gavin Williams and Carl Fletcher, they were never going to be regulars when West Ham went up. The worry was that if we got promotion, we might have players who would not be up to the required standard.

Charlton released eight players, including three significant first-team players. Hasselbaink left, which was no great loss after a very disappointing season; he managed only two league goals, which for someone who averaged about fifteen goals a season is incredibly poor. Apart from the lack of goals, Hasselbaink did not even offer much of a goal threat; the rocket of a right foot seemed to have deserted him. It was also good to get him off the wage bill as we had to bear the cost of relegation.

Talal El Karkouri and Kevin Lisbie were also released. Elk in his first season had contributed a few goals and looked the making of a good player. However, in the relegation year, his performances were inconsistent. After playing in all but four of our games, he has to take some of the blame for our poor defensive record. Some of his performances were just not good enough. Elk was probably better in the opposition's box, so he was another player who would not be missed. Maybe if he had been tried in midfield where his passing range and sharp shooting could have been utilised, this would have been more fruitful.

Kevin Lisbie had never been able to establish himself as first choice; and for someone with good pace and strength, his goal returns were not good enough.

Kevin never fulfilled his potential, which was shown when he scored a fantastic hat trick against Liverpool in 2003. In this game his third goal was one of the goals of the season, a fantastic run and shot into the corner. Lisbie had played on loan for a number of clubs in the Championship and done well; so I thought he would be an asset, but obviously he needed regular football, and even in the second tier this was not guaranteed. Lisbie would be lining up against us as Colchester opted to sign him as they needed to fill the void left by Jamie Cureton and Chris Iwelumo, who ended up at the Valley.

Hermann Hreidarsson activated a relegation clause and left for Portsmouth; he would be missed as since he arrived in 2003, H.H. had established himself as a regular in defence and a firm favourite. Despite not being so solid in the last season, H.H. had been one of our consistent better performers since signing. Hermann knew Portsmouth would be a great opportunity for him to get Premiership first-team football, so it was no surprise to see him go. Pompey fans would surely have been sceptical about signing another defender from Charlton as only six months before they had landed Traore. Also Hreidarsson had a poor record in terms of relegation. At Palace, Wimbledon, Ipswich and now Charlton, H.H. had been part of the defence.

Radostin Kishishev and Bryan Hughes also left the club; neither had been regulars in the last season but would have been more likely to have made an impression in the Championship for us. Hughes had scored some important goals, notably against Palace in 2005 and Villa in Pardew's first win, but was not a game-changing player and did not always make much of an impression in the top league.

Kish especially would be missed as he had been with the club a long time and earned many plaudits for his all action style and phenomenal work rate. A guy who used to sit behind me at Charlton thought that he was a 'fucking idiot' as he was not the most technically gifted of players. But Kish did things not many people noticed, and when he played he was as valuable as anyone. In one game against Birmingham, he lost ten pounds due to his endeavour, which shows how hard he worked.

Dennis Rommedahl unsurprisingly left; he had publically stated if we were relegated, he would be off. Rommedahl was exceptionally talented but did not show it enough. When Ajax signed him, the thought was he would probably be better suited to the less-demanding Dutch league. After seeing him torment France in the World Cup 2002 and do well for Ajax after Charlton, it was a huge pity that he proved a flop at the Valley.

The other two players who left were the most notable and unsurprising departures: Young and Darren Bent. Luke Young, who had England caps to his name and felt he may have a shout of Euro 2008 (if England qualified), needed to be in the Premiership and left for Middlesbrough. Luke Young had been signed for around £4 million in 2001 but was our first choice right back in his six years and deservedly won player of the year in 2005.

Darren Bent left for Tottenham for more than £16 million. Not bad considering we spent £2.5 million only two years before to sign him from Ipswich. The money received was the only positive as Darren would be sorely missed, averaging almost one in two in the top league.

There was the feeling if he stayed Bent could get to twenty-five goals with no problem and give us a great chance to storm the division and be back where we belong.

At one point it looked as though Bent would stay. West Ham had a similar bid to Spurs accepted, but Bent declined to talk to them. For a short while it materialized that maybe we could have held onto him. If there was not a major tournament at the end of the year, who knows?

It seemed strange that he chose Spurs over West Ham as Spurs had Berbatov, Keane and Defoe on their books, so first-team football was not guaranteed. Also there were the Euros at the end of the season, so regular Premiership football was a must.

When in 2006 Eriksson opted to take only four strikers to Germany, Andy Johnson must have rued staying at Palace in the second tier after their relegation. If he had been playing and scoring in the Premiership, he would have had a great shout at being included in the squad. Bent must have thought about this when deciding to leave the Valley. England of course failed to qualify for Euro 2008, but judging by his record since 2005, Bent would again surely have had a shot at playing. Even though Bent would be sorely missed, the money we received was very good, and his reasons for leaving were more than understandable.

Iain Dowie spent two years' budget the year before, and even though Pardew would not have the luxury to spend that much money, the Bent deal allowed us to bring in some reinforcements. Alan Pardew had done well in the January window, but now was his big chance to improve our squad. I must admit the players Pardew brought in seemed impressive and more than capable of fitting in well.

Paddy McCarthy signed from Leicester for less than a million. He had the reputation for being a no-nonsense defender and looked as though he could form a good partnership with Bougherra. McCarthy clearly had good leadership qualities and was a potential captain after Bent and Young had left. We also signed Yassin Moutaouakil as another defensive option. Yassin was an unknown but was the French U21 captain, so he seemed a good acquisition. With Luke Young gone, we needed a right back to compete with young Sankofa, who'd done well in the Premiership.

The other notable defender brought in was the legendary Chris Powell for his third spell at the club. Even though Powell would probably not play regularly due to his age, every Charlton fan was pleased to see him return. Powell had always given 100 per cent for us and was rewarded with England recognition in 2001. If it were not for the emergence of Ashley Cole, there would have been the possibility of his playing at the World Cup in 2002. Two things were clear: if needed, Chris would not let the side down and would always play with a wide trademark smile. With Powell returning there was also the likelihood that he would begin his coaching career and maybe have a significant role to play off the pitch as well.

In midfield there were not so many new faces. Dean Sinclair arrived from Barnet, but it was unclear whether he was seen as a first-team regular. Similarly Thierry Racon also signed from France. But the significant signing was Zheng Zhi on a permanent contract. This was a great coup for Charlton as it was widely reported that he would sign for a Premiership club after impressing during his loan spell. Zheng looked good enough to make a difference in the top league, so to have him in the Championship was fantastic.

Similarly to Yassin we also signed Jose Semedo, a Portuguese youngster who was a bit of an unknown but could play in defence or midfield. Semedo had played for the Portuguese Under 21s and been part of the same youth set up that produced Figo and Ronaldo, so he obviously had quality.

Scott Carson had returned to Liverpool as expected, so we needed a new keeper. Even though Randolph had done well on loan at Accrington Stanley, he was only twenty, so there was need for some experience. The man chosen was a surprise: Nicky Weaver As I mentioned he was not a favourite at the Valley but was a talented keeper who would have surely played for England had he not had so many horrendous injuries. I am not sure if every Charlton fan was pleased with the signing of Weaver, but you have to credit him for choosing Charlton when there would surely have been other offers. Immediately Nicky expressed his desire to win over the fans; certainly Charlton could have done a lot worse than Weaver.

It was up front where there was the most change. obviously Darren Bent, Lisbie and Hasselbaink left. To replace them we spent big on Luke Varney and Izale McLeod. Both had done very well in the lower league for Crewe and MK Dons, respectively, and looked more than capable of the step up. Varney and McLeod had scored goals for fun and both had pace to burn. Even though we spent more than £4 million on them, they seemed good investments. Varney in particular had attracted interest from the Premiership, so this was a good coup for the club.

We also signed the experienced pair Svetoslav Todorov and Chris Iwelumo on free transfers. Todorov had played in Portsmouth's title-winning campaign in 2003 and gave us another option. He scored for fun when Pompey went up. If it hadn't been for a long-term injury after promotion, he would surely have done well in the Premiership.

Similarly Iwelumo had done very well at Colchester, including for a spell under our assistant manager Phil Parkinson, and would provide another option up front as he was the typical target man and had plenty of promotional experience with the likes of Stoke and Brighton. Iwelumo did not have much pace but knew the Championship inside out and would give us another dimension.

It seemed unlikely that one of the earlier signings of Pardew's tenure, Chris Dickson, would be a regular and would most probably go to a League One club on loan to get some league experience. Dickson signed just after the transfer window in early 2007 so could only play in the reserves until the new season. He signed from non-league Dulwich Hamlet after scoring hatfuls of goals. Even though he would probably go on loan judging by the fact he had scored a few for our reserves, there was the possibility we had unearthed a gem. Comparisons were being drawn with Ian Wright, who also came into the professional game late; the prospect was certainly an exciting one.

In the lead up to the opening game, another one of Dowie's signings left: Diawara, which was a shame in my opinion as in the last half of the season, he really looked a top defender. In his last twelve games for the club, we conceded only nine goals (hardly relegation form) and had a good run of clean sheets. It was no coincidence that away at Blackburn when things fell apart and we got a thumping, Diawara was unavailable.

It seemed as though Pardew had assembled a quality squad, Andy Reid had pledged his future to the club and would hopefully stay fit. If he could he would provide Premiership class. Reid was named captain, not the natural choice in my opinion as I was sure McCarthy or Matt Holland would receive the armband. The extra responsibility showed that he was going to be the main man.

Pardew had adopted a similar policy to when he was at West Ham, and they had been promoted. It seemed as though even before a ball had been kicked, Pardew had spent his money better than Dowie did. In fact I would go so far as to say in many ways, maybe minus Darren Bent, our squad in 2007 was better equipped for the Premiership than it was a year before. There seemed to be more strength in depth and certainly more options up front. On impressive element as well was players now who looked as though they could be assets if we got promoted. Alan Pardew had not signed players just for the Championship. Albeit prematurely there was the likelihood if we got promotion, the squad would not need a complete transformation as the foundations were already there.

Relegation really hit home when the fixtures were announced. First up was Scunthorpe at home. When talking about the Championship the year before, the thought was that if we went down, we would have to go to places like Scunthorpe and Blackpool. The year before we had travelled across London to Upton Park and then had Manchester United visiting the Valley. What a difference a year makes. Nevertheless, the feeling was that a home start was good, and Scunthorpe represented a good chance to make a winning start.

During both relegation years, people commented that relegation would mean we would see Charlton win more. Judging by our opening fixtures when we were not due to play any of our predicted promotion challengers, the games did look favourable. Of course the hope was these would provide a great opportunity to stop any relegation hangover and lay down a marker.

Not that there was a good time to be relegated, but this year because of the increased revenue, Charlton were missing out heavily. When you see the promoted sides such as Sunderland spending big (£9 million on Gordon and £5 million on Chopra) it really does hit home about what we were losing. If we had stayed up and held onto Darren Bent and some of the others, we could have built a really strong squad. With plans to increase the Valley to 40,000, Charlton could have established themselves up with the likes of Spurs and West Ham as top London clubs.

West Ham were reaping the benefits of surviving as they spent big. Charlton fans were getting excited by players from the MK Dons whilst West Ham were signing players from Liverpool and Arsenal; they also had England international Dean Ashton finally getting back to fitness. Curbs finally had the money he should have had at Charlton. In 2007 it was too late to be bitter, but seeing Curbs buy Bellamy and Parker filled Charlton fans with envy.

Normally in a season one team suffers a Premiership relegation hangover and struggles to adapt to the Championship. After seven years in the top flight, there was the possibility that even with our newly assembled squad we would struggle with the more physical aspect of the division. We were relegated with Sheffield United and Watford, who had much more recent experience of promotion campaigns, so the pessimist in me believed they would be fine in adapting. Sheffield United spent big as well, especially in signing James Beattie for £4 million, so I thought they would be our nearest challengers. Wolves also brought in Freddy Eastwood and looked capable of mounting a charge.

The football magazine *FourFourTwo* usually includes a pull-out in the August edition; here fans of the ninety-two league clubs give their predictions for the season. Two of the questions relate to best- and worst-case scenarios for the year. The Charlton fan said promotion was best, obviously, and worst was that we would end up like Ipswich or Sheffield Wednesday and fall into mid table mediocrity in the Championship. In all honesty it seems hard to imagine this happening. With a talented squad, things would have to go very wrong for us not to be challenging near the top.

One thing that I was also confident on was Pardew being the right man for the job; he nearly saved us from the drop and looked like he had acquired the players to ensure a swift return. In preseason the strikers had scored goals, and the other new players looked as though they were bedding in well.

Or final warm-up game was against Braga from Portugal. They beat us, but we were not embarrassed. Ambrose, who could have left, scored a fine goal. Braga were managed by ex-Charlton player Jorge Costa, who was a favourite in his short spell with the club. Costa had been out of favour at Porto so came to Charlton to play games before the 2002 World Cup. At the time this was a major coup for the club. Despite being a loan, he fitted in perfectly, and it would have been great to keep him longer. Unfortunately he went back to Porto and won numerous trophies there.

Jorge Costa made his debut for Charlton in December 2001 as we won at Stamford Bridge. The game after, he helped keep Teddy Sheringham quiet in another win against Spurs. This year our record against London sides was amongst the best. The week after he returned to the Valley, we were playing Scunthorpe in the Championship.

The Scunthorpe game was in the end a massive disappointment; we fully deserved to win but could not finish and drew 1–1. Marcus Bent, who had repeatedly been linked with other clubs, scored for us but then lost his marker at a corner to allow them an equalizer. The one problem with being favourites is that the other sides see you as a scalp and tend to raise their game when playing you.

This was certainly the case with Scunthorpe. The match had almost a cup-tie feel to it as with respect playing at a ground like the Valley for many of their players was a day out. They were not expecting much as for some of them to play at a Premiership stadium was a once-in-a-career opportunity. Scunthorpe looked an average side but were spirited and worked hard. As favourites to go down drawing at our place was a scalp for them, but nine times out of ten we would have beaten them easily.

After they had scored, Scunthorpe decided to waste as much time as possible. This did not affect the result but would be a common feature of teams visiting the Valley not expecting to win. Every team does it when they are holding on and it is late, but the referee should have tried to hurry the game up and let it flow better.

A number of debutants played that day. Yassin Moutaouakil especially stood out and won man of the match. He completely unknown, and it looked as though Charlton had struck gold with Yassin. He set up our goal, and all afternoon was a constant threat to Scunthorpe with marauding runs up and down the right-hand side. Mouts also looked lightening quick, and even though Scunthorpe did not offer great attacking threats, most home fans had forgotten about Luke Young.

Of course it is wrong to assess whether a player will be a success on the basis of one game, but Mouts looked the part. Weaver and McCarthy looked solid, and Semedo in midfield looked very tidy. Zheng's transfer had only just gone through, so he was unavailable for the match. Varney was injured, so there was quality to come back. It would obviously take time to establish who would be regulars and the different partnerships, particularly up front where there was clearly an abundance of quality.

Our first away trip of the season was to be televised from Stoke. This game was a welcome to the Championship. Despite Andy Reid putting us in front, we struggled afterwards and Stoke won 2–1. To make matters worse, Mouts picked up an injury which ruled him out for a while. The performance at Stoke was nowhere near good enough as we were bullied and could not handle their physical nature. Stoke may have been criticised for their style of play, but it works, and this afternoon to great effect.

In 2008–9 Stoke did very well in surprising everyone and staying up comfortably in the Premiership. Even though they do not play the best free-flowing football, they do get results. If Stoke attempted to pass the ball around, they would surely not be so successful. West Brom were also promoted with Stoke, and they do play nice football but can't put the ball in the net. Stoke may ruffle a few feathers but are still quite exciting to watch.

On the afternoon we lost at Stoke, if we hadn't know before, it was evident now that the Championship would be hard and we would have to change our style a bit to avoid being bullied out of games. It was only two games gone, and against Scunthorpe we deserved to win. So in terms of negativity, we were a way off the previous December. The newspaper reports the day after were not favourable, particularly as in both games we had been in front and given up the lead far too quickly.

To be 2–0 was hugely disappointing. The defending had been bad, and it was clear we needed someone at right back to fill in for Yassin. Finally in our third game, we got our first win, and it was a welcome relief. After being 2–0 down at half-time to Sheffield Wednesday, we fought back to win 3–2 with a couple of the new players making big differences. At half-time Marcus Bent came off for Todorov, and we staged a fine fight back, Andy Reid scoring a fine goal with his weaker right foot to give us hope, and then two fine goals from Iwelumo on his full debut ensured the win. The goals from Iwelumo were both fine finishes with his right foot. This was a surprise as he was more noted for his heading ability but had shown this was not the case. At 2–1 when we were chasing the leveller, Weaver made a terrific save to deny them a third, which would have probably killed us off. It turned out this was a pivotal save and, I am sure, helped to silence some of Weaver's doubters. The main thing was that we had our first win and had shown fantastic qualities such as determination and spirit. It was also good to see Iwelumo off the mark.

During the next week, we were involved in a fantastic Carling Cup tie with Stockport, where some of the fringe players got a chance to impress. Todorov scored a brilliant goal on the turn to get off the mark while Zheng also opened his account. A 4–3 win was certainly hard earned, but there were some good positives to come from the game. Darren Randolph made his home debut in goal, and despite letting in three goals, it is hard to lay any blame at his door. Just as at Liverpool the previous May, he looked an able deputy if Weaver were to get injured.

Despite this there was more important news at the club this week: Marcus Bent left the club to join Wigan for the season on loan. A friend of mine, Tom, believes Marcus would have scored goals regularly in the Championship and been a good player to keep. I was pleased to see him go, especially with the strikers we had signed. Two and half million pounds is a lot for a striker who does not score goals. Despite playing well on his own up front when Darren was injured in early 2007, one league goal all season is poor. Since he was possibly on Premiership wages, to get him off the wage bill was a good thing.

The Dowie legacy decreased even more with the departure of Amady Faye. As with other Dowie signings, there were no tears shed at his going to Rangers albeit on loan. He had not replicated his Portsmouth form, which prompted Newcastle to spend big on him, and he ultimately proved another Dowie flop. It was only a loan move for the year, but we all thought it was the last we saw of Shamdy Faye, as he was nicknamed by some fans.

Our final pieces of business surrounded two defenders: Sodje and Mills. Sam Sodje, who had done well in League One, for Brentford arrived on loan from Reading after struggling to cement a place. One of our former players, the controversial figure Danny Mills, arrived on loan from Man City. Mills had done very well for Charlton in his first spell playing in the Premiership before signing for Leeds for £4 million; not bad business at all. Even though he was booed when he returned with Leeds and City, most Charlton fans were pleased to see him back at the club and knew he would give his all. The defence now had more of a solid look, and were injuries or suspensions would not affect us too badly.

The Wednesday match was already a highlight as getting our season properly started, but our fourth game away at Palace was one that sticks out massively. It was our first meeting since we sent Palace down in 2005. No doubt there would have been an interesting atmosphere in the boardroom because our chairman and fan Richard Murray apparently rather enjoyed the match in 2005 which angered their chairman Simon Jordan.

Jordan may have been proved right with his comments regarding 'What goes around, comes around' as we were now in the same division as Palace was. As a Charlton fan, I cannot blame Murray for lapping up the fact we sent Palace down. It may not have been in the best taste, but Murray was only doing what 25,000 others were doing that day, and somehow I don't believe Murray went as far as going around the boardroom singing 'We sent the Palace down'.

Bill Kenwright is a massive Everton fan, and if a similar situation were to occur with Everton and Liverpool, it is hard to imagine the people in charge at Liverpool acting in a way Simon Jordan has and referring to their fans as morons or being disrespectful to Kenwright.

I was not at the Palace away game, choosing instead to watch *Soccer Saturday*. By all accounts it was an even match, but we sneaked it near the end thanks to Todorov. The goal was a good finish after a defensive mix-up, but we had beaten our rivals again at Selhurst Park thanks to a late goal. It was fantastic to see Toddy get his first league goal and a good response from him after being dropped to the bench.

As was now a Sunday routine, I watched the Championship – this week the Palace match was the featured game. This made a change from *Match of the Day*, where usually Charlton would be one of the last teams shown. Watching the highlights, I saw that clearly Weaver had again shown his class with some fine saves and Iwelumo had led the line well. Finally Chris Powell and Danny Mills made their third and second league debuts for us and looked solid as ever. After a shaky start, we had bounced back with two good wins, and it seemed as though we were getting used to the Championship. Despite only four games gone, the new players had settled in well, and to get one over our nearest and dearest so early was a major boost.

Chapter 7

Bouncing Back

Following a good win against Palace, we travelled to Colchester in high hopes. Even though Layer Road was a tricky place to go, Charlton were favourites. Colchester had overachieved the previous year with our own Iwelumo up front but had signed Lisbie and Teddy Sheringham so looked a good bet for another good season.

This was to be the final season that Colchester would play at Layer Road before moving to a new all-seater stadium. Having been there a few seasons before for a friendly, I saw that it was clear they needed to move as Layer Road had only a small capacity and was not up to the standard seen in the Championship. The season before, Colchester had made their home a fortress, so there was no way it was going to be easy. But there was the chance our big money signing Luke Varney would make his debut after an injury.

Varney had been prolific for Crewe and looked like a good replacement for Darren Bent. Even though Toddy and Iwelumo had done well since signing, to see Varney in the squad was a big boost, and many fans saw him as the main man up front.

After forty minutes we were 2–0 down. No surprise in who scored for Colchester: Lisbie carrying on his good start to the season and proving a point to Alan Pardew. The defending had been a bit shambolic, even though Sheringham had been instrumental in their first, but again we showed good resilience to come back. Toddy got his third goal in three games, and then late on Zheng fired in a well-deserved equaliser. After coming back from two down again, I was a bit disappointed with only a point, especially as Colchester were reduced to ten men. But it was clear the team had spirit and guts.

It seemed that Charlton were developing Jekyll-and-Hyde tendencies, certainly according to the Charlton Web site. At the back we were conceding silly goals but were scoring plenty, and our quality was shining through when it mattered. Again at Colchester Nicky Weaver had made some good saves. As in the Wednesday game, a save at 2–1 proved vital.

Two home games followed, both against former Premier League sides in Norwich and Leicester. Neither had started the season particularly well, so we felt a good return was more than possible. First up was Norwich on a Tuesday night. If we won there was the chance to go into third. Danny Mills and Chris Powell would make their home debuts at the back whilst Varney would make his full debut alongside Iwelumo.

In the end we won 2–0, two late penalties, both from Andy Reid, ensuring a good home win. We should have won the game by the time we were awarded the first. Only the woodwork and good goalkeeping kept it 0–0. There were many positives from the game. Luke Varney worked hard up front and despite not scoring was unlucky not to open his account whilst our seemingly forgotten man, Izale McLeod, came on and changed the game. McLeod won both penalties impressively, showing his pace and strength. Our squad was already looking very strong, and to have a player such as McLeod coming off the bench to such good effect was excellent to see.

Lloyd Sam also had a fine game on the right. After threatening to break into the side before, this was to be a big season for Sam. Blessed with good pace and trickery, Lloyd had all the attributes to be a fine winger. He just needed to be more consistent with final delivery. But against Norwich he was a big threat down the right.

Danny Mills certainly announced his arrival back at the club with an all-action display against one of his former sides. He had a good tussle with Huckerby all night and was determined to silence the Norwich boos. Danny Mills is not everyone's cup of tea and certainly does not mind upsetting the opposition, but you cannot say he is not a good right back. Mills played at the World Cup in 2002 and in the Champions League for Leeds, so there is a lot of talent alongside the controversy. Here he was lucky not to get booked but stifled Huckerby well. His winding up predictably boiled over in the last minutes when Dion Dublin was red-carded for a clash with Mills.

We went into the Leicester game in good spirits. They had been through some managerial turmoil, with Martin Allen lasting only a couple of league games and their new manager, Gary Megson, not being the most popular choice. At the Valley we comfortably beat them 2–0, Luke Varney getting off the mark and Big Chris

Iwelumo also finding the net. It was good to see Varney open his account, and the partnership with Chris looked as though it would be successful. A typical little-and-large partnership, with the pace and work rate of Varney and the aerial presence of Iwelumo, against Leicester Charlton had their very own Phillips and Quinn combo.

In midfield Jose Semedo was proving to be a real find, even though he could play at the back, it was in the centre of midfield where he was shining. Even though he had good potential, having played in Portugal and Italy, he had settled in quicker than most would have expected and alongside Reid or Zheng seemed to complement them well with his tenacity and ability to break up the play. Semedo also had a good range of passing. Against Leicester the fans acknowledged his performances, singing his name late in the second half.

One thing that surprised me was that Norwich and Leicester had been in the top flight only a few years previously but both came to the Valley and looked anything but Premiership sides. Despite the fact Charlton were amongst the favourites to go up so teams would understandably not go all out attack, neither side looked as though they had come to the Valley realistically expecting to win. Weaver had to make one or two decent saves but was hardly overworked in the two games.

After the Colchester game, Paddy McCarthy had been dropped, and Bougherra and Fortune started to form a partnership at the back. Bougherra had not played much in the Premiership and was beginning to look the part. It seemed as though they complemented each other well. Jon Fortune had been with the club a long time and had the chance to leave in the summer but had decided to stay and fight for a first-team place. Credit must go to him for this as Stoke probably would have offered him guaranteed football, but he had started the season well for us, and after losing Diawara, I was pleased he stayed.

Our next away game in the league certainly had some spice to it, against Iain Dowie's Coventry City. During the week before, Coventry had beaten Man United in the Carling Cup whilst Luton had knocked us out. Being knocked out by Luton was no bad thing. A cup run is always nice, but having started the season well, we knew the league was very important and the last thing we needed was more injuries.

Against Dowie's team we played well and probably deserved the win, but a late equaliser denied us. A win would have taken us to top of the league as Watford could also only draw, but a point away was still respectable. In the game we were the victims of a poor refereeing decision. Luke Varney went through and was clearly taken down by their defender, but the ref waived away our appeals. It was a certain penalty and probably a red-card offence. But a point maintained our good start to the season, and to be two points off top spot so early on was impressive.

Surprisingly Sheffield United were struggling to adapt to the Championship, and despite having very talented players and Bryan Robson in charge, of the three relegated sides, they were the ones with the hangover. Watford on the other hand were flying Their promotion was perhaps a season too soon as they had players not good enough for the Premiership, but like us in 1999–0 they had kept hold of their key players, especially Marlon King and Danny Shittu.

Aside from the other relegated sides, the teams that lost in the playoffs – including West Brom and Wolves (who'd spent a fair amount themselves) – also looked strong in the early weeks. We knew West Brom would be near the top. They'd been unlucky in the playoffs the previous May and had some very talented players. Kevin Phillips was almost guaranteed twenty goals a season, and like us with Zheng, they'd done well to keep onto players like Zoltan Gera. Bristol City, who'd been promoted only that year, were also doing well. There was plenty of quality at the top, and even this early it seemed as though no one was going to run away with the league.

When you get relegated, there are always away trips that are not relished, for example, Hull City away on a Tuesday night. Despite my poor away record, this is the sort of game I would have thoroughly enjoyed. It is the sign of a real football fan if you are prepared to go to Hull on a wet Tuesday. Unfortunately I could not persuade any friends or family to make the trip, so I had to rely on Sky.

Away at Hull there were a few reunions. Phil Parkinson, our assistant, had an unhappy managerial spell there the year before. Also in the Hull line up, Bryan Hughes and Michael Turner both had strong Charlton connections. When in the Premiership, we had let go a number of younger players. Some have formed good careers in the lower leagues and had not been missed, but Turner certainly is a regrettable loss as he had gone on to be a top defender and surely would have been an asset if we had kept him. Turner is now a regular in the top flight and has been linked with a big move and an England call-up. Our selling him to Brentford seems in hindsight a big mistake.

The match itself was very dramatic. We won 2–1, Varney and Iwelumo scoring again, but before half-time both sides had a player sent off. Lloyd Sam and Ashbee were involved in a nasty tussle. It seemed as though the red for Sam looked harsh, and this was shown by our appeal (it was rejected). Following the game the FA charged both sides for failing to control their players. This coupled with ten minutes of added time, made watching Sky very tense, especially as all the other games had been finished for a good few minutes.

After two good home wins in September, our first home game – against a Barnsley side widely tipped to struggle – looked like a home banker. The only downside going into the game was the loss of Lloyd Sam to suspension as he'd been playing really well and looked one of the best wingers in the league.

Like the Scunthorpe game, this one proved immensely frustrating. Andy Reid seemed to be making hitting the bar his speciality. Reid had been fantastic early on in the season but had been very unlucky not to have more goals. Also goalkeepers must have enjoyed playing at the Valley as Muller in the Barnsley goal was not the first keeper to have a blinder.

After dominating the game, finally Zheng scored with less than ten minutes to go. But yet again we threw it away and could even have lost. Barnsley equalized with a minute to go after some poor defending, and then McCann should have won it when he went through one on one. Strangely after scoring late, we seemingly got nervous and started to defend far too deep.

Despite not losing one could not help but feel very disappointed at the result. It was another game where we had thrown away the lead to a team that we should have beaten comfortably Barnsley were nothing special but had effectively stolen a point. When walking away from the Valley listening to the away fans singing 'It's just like watching Brazil', I felt sick that we had missed a good chance to win another home game. Even this early on, it seemed possible that these points dropped could be vital, especially as we had not really played any of the sides near the top and not had a real test yet.

During the following week, Chris Dickson scored a hat trick for Gillingham, where he was on loan. Earlier in the season his loan at Crewe had not worked out, but this move he had hit the ground running. Watching the goals on Sky Sports, I thought it seemed as though when he returned, there would be another striker pushing for a first-team place.

Alan Pardew had talked of the importance of young players coming through. Obviously Lloyd Sam had started to establish himself, and a couple of younger players had been doing well on loan. Grant Basey and Josh Wright, like Dickson, looked as though they could have a say in first-team matters when they returned from Brentford and Barnet, respectively.

The future of Charlton was looking bright again. In the early 2000s, a number of players came through and did very well; Scott Parker being the most successful, but Jon Fortune and Paul Konchesky also were products of our system. With the financial implications of dropping out of the top flight, it was good to see players coming through who were capable of playing in the Championship or maybe even higher.

There was an international break after the Barnsley. Interesting news from our rivals Palace broke during the two weeks that Neil Warnock was their new manager. Their old manager, Peter Taylor, had struggled to match the fans' ambitions, and our win at Selhurst Park a month or so earlier had put him under pressure. The outspoken chairman Jordan opted to go with the equally outspoken Warnock, a marriage made in heaven.

Warnock had left Sheffield United after they joined us in being relegated from the Premiership; he had a fantastic record for getting sides promoted. However, Crystal Palace were nearer to the relegation zone, and there would have to be a major turnaround if they were to challenge us for promotion. The worry was though that if any manager could do it, it would be Warnock.

On the Saturday we played for the first time in a game against a side also expected to be challenging, Wolves. This was the start of a difficult week for Charlton as we lost three on the bounce for the first time in almost a year and lost a key player with a season-long injury.

Jay Bothroyd scored the opener for Wolves, typical after playing for us under Curbs. When Bothroyd left at the same time as players such as Johansson, there was no real upset. He had scored a few goals, notably in the cups, but was not good enough for the Premier League and never fulfilled the potential he showed early on at Arsenal.

At Wolves we did not play too badly but missed our chances and did not defend well when it mattered. Also in this game Chris Powell and Darren Ambrose left the game with injuries, which did not help. It was our first defeat since the second game, and with two home games on the bounce, it felt like a blip.

On the Tuesday it was a case of Charlton versus Rob Styles rather than Plymouth. We did more than enough to win the game but found another goalkeeper in good form and a referee who wanted to overshadow the players. Before the kickoff when the referee's name was announced, Styles cupped his hand to his ear. This summed up his professionalism. What referee normally does this before a game? Before this game I saw Styles like most refs – not great, but not bad. He certainly was not in the same league as Graham Poll for Mr Ego, but in this game it seemed at times that Styles was almost enjoying upsetting everyone as well as being centre of attention.

Svetoslav Todorov was the victim of an awful challenge by a Plymouth defender which caused Toddy to rupture the cruciate ligament in his knee, ruling him out for the season. This was a massive loss as Todorov had already scored some vital goals. His experience would surely be missed. In a match where Styles gave ten yellow cards, Timar, the player responsible for the injury, did not even get a yellow. Ian Holloway, the Plymouth boss, said he was surprised that he did not get a caution.

For the rest of the match, especially in the second half when we were trying to get the equaliser, Rob Styles did all he could to slow the game down and frustrate both sides. Many of the bookings were for dissent or shows of petulance, such as kicking the ball away, which sums up how much his performance infuriated the players.

One thing evident about the Championship was that teams were happy to come to the Valley and waste time playing for a draw. Certainly this was the case with

Scunthorpe and Barnsley. Obviously this goes on in every division and is a fact of football. No doubt when Charlton went to the bigger teams in the Premiership, we were happy to put ten men behind the ball. But you often need the referee to try to let the rest of the game flow to avoid long pauses and breaks in play. Rob Styles was very whistle happy, and in a match that was not particularly dirty (except for the Timar challenge) he was determined to keep stopping play.

I am not saying that Styles was the reason we lost – our own poor defending and their keeper contributed to this – but it was one of the worst displays by a referee I have seen in a long while. Graham Poll and his assistants massively cost us in Pardew's first game, but that was one awful decision Against Plymouth the whole game was littered with poor refereeing.

To lose our first match of the season at home was majorly disappointing. We had a makeshift back four. With Danny Mills at left back, Luke Varney had to play on the right of midfield as Ambrose had joined the casualties. But this did not change the fact we did not play well. The defending for both goals was very poor, allowing Ebanks-Blake the freedom of the penalty box to put them in front before stupidly giving the ball away on the edge of the area. The second goal seemed to trickle into the goal in slow motion. In the second half, Iwelumo was guilty of a glaring miss, and McLeod was ineffective up front. All round the performance was substandard.

Reading the reports the next day, I saw there was another sub-plot to the game surrounding their keeper Luke McCormick. During the season in the Valley match day programme, there had been a feature from a scout on the opposition. Against Plymouth the scout had reported that McCormick was not the best on crosses. McCormick apparently read this and then typically went on to have a fine game. Ian Holloway made a point of bringing this up after the match. It was then decided that this feature would not reappear.

QPR were next up, and as they were bottom of the league, it seemed the perfect chance to bounce back and put the difficult week behind us. Lloyd Sam would be back from suspension, and Luke Varney would go back up front after playing out of position against Argyle. Grant Basey had returned from his loan, and with no other fit recognised left back, he made his debut against QPR.

As it turned out, Basey's debut was the only positive in another disappointing game. QPR won 1–0, but it could have been more. Surely when after half-time they missed a penalty, it should have been a warning sign, but we could not really get started. Basey did well at left back, but the rest of the side put in another below-par performance.

The goal that won the game had an element of controversy as it looked as though Weaver was fouled before Bolder stabbed home. It was the type of coming together that normally results in a free kick to the goalkeeper, followed by people saying keepers are overprotected. Here though it looked as though the striker had his arms all over Weaver, and surely if he hadn't, the keeper would have claimed. However, we deserved to lose the game. After a very good start, three defeats and bad performances in a week were poor. In a matter of seven days, we had gone from second to eighth.

Understandably the team was booed off at the end, and fans' frustrations built as this was the fourth home game of the season which we'd failed to win against a side that we should have beaten.

Despite a bad run, Pardew came out and apologized for the QPR game, taking responsibility for moving Reid into the centre, hoping this would make a difference. It would have been easy to blame the referee for the goal, but Pardew was not shirking his responsibility, and this sent out a positive message.

After a poor October, the first four games in November could not have gone better as against good opposition we deservedly won all four and sent out a real message that we were up for the challenge and could mount a real challenge.

The first game away at Southampton was probably one of our most impressive performances and results of the season. Watching *Soccer Saturday*, I found it difficult not to fear the worst when after thirty-five minutes, Semedo was sent off for two bookings. Normally over the years when we'd been reduced to ten, the best we could hope for would be a draw, and at 0–0 with almost an hour to play, this was certainly the case here.

However after a solid defensive display when Weaver surprisingly did not have too much to do, in the last minute Iwelumo scored a brilliant goal. Luke Varney ran down the right and put in a peach of a cross which Iwelumo powered in to give us an unlikely victory. It was the kind of goal that Iwelumo would score every week if the service to him was good.

Against Southampton we had played with a new 4–5–1 formation, with Iwelumo on his own up front.

This could have seemed negative; however, this gave Andy Reid to offer more support to the front man and allowed us to have two out-and-out wingers. Andy Reid had been our most consistent performer but was always more effective in the centre. He had the ability to unlock a defence and be our most creative player, especially with Todorov out for the season. This change seemed to enable Reid to have more of an influence.

When we were in the Premiership under Curbs, a move to 4–5–1 in 2004 proved to be instrumental in a good run of form. Also at the start of 2005–6 with Darren Bent on his own, we had also done very well. On both occasions Jerome Thomas was on the left and had played some of his best football since joining from Arsenal. Against Southampton he was back in the side, which was quite pleasing. At the start of the season, Jerome had been linked with a Premiership move, but to keep him was a boost as surely he would be one of the better wingers in the league.

The following Tuesday we played away at Bristol City. Judging by the reports on Sky, we played very well but couldn't score. Yet again in the last minute, Iwelumo scored with a cracking header, this time from a Reid cross. Bristol City were second, so to go to Ashton Gate where they'd not lost all season and win was a fantastic result. However, for the second time in four days, when in the last minute, the presenter on Sky had said there'd been a goal in our game, my heart skipped a beat. Against Saints I was sure that the goal had gone against us as surely with seconds to go we'd be defending or trying to keep the ball rather than going for goal. Then against Bristol City after scoring late on the Saturday, it seemed improbable that we'd do it again.

On the Saturday we played Jimmy Floyd Hasselbaink's Cardiff. After some good away wins, it was vital we carry on our good form and improve our home record. Hasselbaink predictably got a frosty reception from the home fans after he probably had the worst season of his career at the Valley. Also he was widely associated with Dowie's regime, so there was no love lost on his return.

I felt sure he would score on his return to silence the boos. In his time at the club, we rarely saw his famous rocket of a right foot, but on this Saturday he lined up a free kick and only a good save from Weaver denied him showing us what we'd missed out on. Just before half-time we continued our run of scoring in injury time with two goals. Sam Sodje scored his first before Iwelumo fired home from outside the box to carry on his good run.

In the second half, the Cardiff fans turned on their manager. They had had a mixed start to the season, and with players such as Hasselbaink and Robbie Fowler in their squad, their fans believed the team should be doing better. Dave Jones had done a fine job there, but it seemed certain that his days were numbered; ironically he kept his job and got them to the FA Cup final. I am certain as the team lined up at Wembley few Cardiff fans wanted a change.

Zheng Zhi scored a fine headed goal near the end to put the gloss on a good performance; 3–0 may have flattered us slightly, but we were back into second. The three defeats had not been completely forgotten; but we had responded very well, so going into the international break we looked a good bet again. Pardew said that we could still get better, which was good to hear. He believed there was far more to come from our squad. Pardew was continuing to make the right noises regarding the rest of the season. Every Charlton fan must have been optimistic that if we could keep player fit, come May we'd be there.

The international break rather than being a welcome break from Charlton, was equally, if not more, frustrating. On the Saturday there was great news from Israel of all places where they beat Russia to mean England needed only a point against Croatia to ensure qualification for Euro 2008. Surely England at home would get the point needed, especially as Croatia had already qualified. Scott Carson was rumoured to be playing after making his England debut on the Friday in a friendly, so the match on the following Wednesday would be more than interesting.

The Sunday after on Sky Sports Yeovil were playing Gillingham. I have to admit even if there were not two Charlton loanees playing, the chances are I would still watch it. James Walker was at Yeovil on loan after not being able to break in at Charlton, and Chris Dickson was still at Gillingham, so it gave the game an extra edge. James Walker scored a cracking winner, but it was Dickson who impressed, scoring his eighth goal in ten games for Gillingham. Eight in ten at any level is impressive, but in League One, the division below Charlton, there was more than enough to suggest he had talent and great goal scoring ability.

Seeing Charlton relegated the year before and playing in some awful games (Wycombe), the England match against Croatia was up there with the most disappointing games I have watched. Scott Carson made a horrendous error to gift Croatia the lead, and then some awful defending put them 2–0 up. Euro 2008 seemed miles away.

England briefly drew level, but then some more poor defending meant Croatia won it 3–2. Russia won their game so England were out. The golden generation had ultimately failed, and Steve McLaren rivalled Les Reed for failure. It was even more disappointing that Carson had played and struggled. Many people forget that Carson actually made one excellent save in the second half, but the damage was done.

The disappointment was obviously massive. If there were the choice between Charlton and England winning, Charlton would win. This result really hurt. Having been unlucky at the World Cup in 2006 with injuries and some bad sportsmanship, Euro 2008 was there for the taking. With Gerrard and Rooney fit and players like Walcott more experienced, we'd surely be amongst the front runners. We'd blown it. I'm sure the FA felt as though they'd blown it by appointing McLaren, especially with some of the other quality managers available at the time.

Our next away game at Preston led to more injury-time goals and another away win. Preston were struggling near the bottom but as QPR had shown us this meant nothing. It was also Alan Irvine's first game in charge for PNE therefore they'd surely have an extra spring in their step. The game was on Sky, so it was a good chance to see us play live and maintain second place.

A lot of credit must go to the players for a 2–0 victory; Zheng Zhi scored a brilliant goal on the turn in first-half injury time before Nicky Weaver probably had his best forty-five minutes in a Charlton shirt. He made two or three excellent saves to preserve the lead, the best save possibly a point blank shot from Sedgwick with twenty minutes to go. In the last minute Luke Varney scored his first for a while with a good goal on the break to seal the points.

Four wins from four was excellent, and the performances had been top notch. Iwelumo had been superb up front whilst four consecutive clean sheets speaks for itself. With two home games up next, we believed that our form could continue and we could carry on putting pressure on Watford, who looked like they were up there for the duration.

The Tuesday night at home to Sheffield United was one of the stranger results of the season. The 3–0 defeat looked like a thrashing, but the game could have gone either way; it really was just one of those nights. At half-time we were a goal down to a penalty stupidly given away by Thomas. Early in the second we missed two sitters, which proved pivotal. The first was from Iwelumo, and even though it was a great save from Kenny, Big Chris should have scored. Zheng then missed an equally good chance but hit the bar when surely it was easier to score.

Iwelumo and Zheng had been superb in recent weeks, so they could be excused an off night, but the defending for Utd's second and third goals was inexcusable. Sheffield United had not made the best start to the season but had chosen the wrong time to show their undoubted quality. With the prolific Beattie up front and player such as Kilgallon and Kenny, they looked as though the playoffs were not beyond possibility.

Against Burnley the defensive problems continued as we conceded two identical goals from set pieces early on to give us a mountain to climb. Going into the game we knew Burnley would be difficult. They had beaten top of the league Watford in mid week, and their new manager, Owen Coyle, was making a name for himself as an up-and-coming boss.

During the game the fans got very restless. We did not play well, and for the first noticeable time this season, we used Iwelumo as someone to just hit the ball at and hope for the best. Iwelumo was a target man, but there was no use every time we got the ball going long and hoping to feed off him. At 2–0 we forced our way back into the game, and were unlucky not to get a leveller. Danny Mills made a massive error, giving away another pathetic penalty which sealed our fate. Another home defeat and another three goals conceded looked awful.

Interestingly in the match-day programme, a Burnley fan had described their striker Andy Gray as the complete Championship striker. Burnley showed us how to properly utilise a target man, such as Gray, and left the Valley with two goals. This would not be the last we'd see of Andy Gray.

Our Jekyll-and-Hyde form continued with two of our better performances of the season. First was away at Cardiff when for the second time in a matter of weeks, we comfortably beat them, this time 2–0. Matt Holland scored a cracking goal from outside the box before Andy Reid capped a great individual performance with a penalty. Even though Cardiff were struggling, a win there was still a good result, and maybe playing away was suiting our style of play more than at home, where fans were quick to lose patience.

Alan Pardew on the Web site and in the media emphasised our home form and the need for improvement starting with Ipswich. Like us Ipswich had been very good at times, especially at home (including a 6–0 victory over second place Bristol City). But their season was even more inconsistent, and with no away wins the game was a great opportunity to improve our patchy home form.

Ipswich were known for playing good football as we were. Jim Magilton had installed a philosophy where getting the ball down would be paramount. Even with Big Chris up front, we had tried to play football the right way rather than lumping the ball, so the Ipswich game would be a decent game.

Alan Pardew kept faith with the 4–5–1 formation but put Andy Reid on the left with Darren Ambrose just behind Iwelumo. It worked a treat, and Darren probably had his best game in a Charlton shirt, scoring two and being a constant threat. At half-time we were 3–0 up and had played some great stuff. Iwelumo scored again, and there were some great individual performers, including Andy Reid.

Darren Ambrose has never been a fan favourite at the Valley despite being one of the first to say he wanted to stay after relegation and some important goals. The problem is he is versatile but has never played consistently well in any position; also some of his weaknesses never helped with the fans. Darren does not have enough pace to play out wide, nor has he made a case to be a centre midfielder. In the hole, as it is often referred to, he looked the player that was worth £5 million only a few years before. When he had played so well for Ipswich and Newcastle, he had played off the striker. This therefore raised the question of why had he constantly been played out wide for us when judging by his performances he was not up to it.

In the second half we were a little nervous; 3–0 will always worry me, and Ipswich like West Ham in February that year as the away side, had a good chance to force their way back into the game with more than forty minutes to play. Nicky Weaver saved us though with a cracking save from a Lee penalty, and we weathered the proverbial storm. Charlton could have added more but missed one or two decent openings. There was also a penalty shout for us, but no luck there.

They pulled one back later through a back heel from Counago. If this had been scored in the Premiership, it would have been replayed over and over. Thierry Henry scored a fine back heel against us one year in a 4–0 win for Arsenal at Highbury. I there to witness such a goal and ever since it has been constantly shown on Sky. Luckily Counago's was just a consolation, and we had got our home form back on track.

The Ipswich game was one of the highlights of the season so far. We played exceptionally well in the first half and looked every inch a top side against a fellow promotion candidate. Going into the vital festive period, we were only a couple of points off top. With West Brom up next, we could be top at Christmas and looked on course for an immediate return to the Promised Land.

Chapter 8

BYE REID, BYE PROMOTION

The fantastic performance and result against Ipswich came at a cost, with two more players in Danny Mills and Jon Fortune joining Lloyd Sam on the suspended list. Danny and Lloyd were to be absent only for the West Brom game after five bookings, but Jon Fortune would be out for three games after a very late red card.

Just as the final whistle went, Fortune lashed out at Alan Lee with an elbow and received a red card. It was very unlike Fortune, whose disciplinary record had always been impressive for a defender. The major disappointment was that he had been playing well and would surely be missed. It meant just as the defence was starting to pick itself, there would be further reshuffle.

If we'd beat West Brom in a lunchtime kickoff, we'd have gone top, at least for a couple of hours. Unfortunately West Brom were just a bit too good for us despite a thoroughly entertaining game. West Brom like Ipswich the week before played some attractive football. Pardew said the match was a fantastic advert for the

Championship. West Brom deserved the victory, but as in our other away defeats, we missed chances at crucial points; notably Luke Varney had a good chance to put us ahead at 2–2 but fluffed his lines.

The injuries cost us as we conceded four sloppy goals; Zoltan Gera scored two similar goals at the back post while Kevin Phillips as he often did scored against us. What seemed strange was that Sankofa did not play after he impressed in the Premiership, and Pardew opted with Semedo at right back. Even though he will always be a legend, Chris Powell showed his age in this game as Gera beat him twice at the back post.

To make matters worse, we lost Andy Reid to a knee-ligament injury ruling him for over a month. Our squad was down to the bare bones as Iwelumo was also taken off at half-time after scoring another fine headed goal. Nevertheless, we had not played badly going forward. Iwelumo had scored his ninth of the season, which was a very good return, whilst Izale McLeod finally got off the mark for the season, which was pleasing. McLeod clearly had a lot of talent, but maybe the price tag had affected him. Also, Pardew had put a lot of pressure on him after he signed, talking of twenty plus goals for the season, which possibly weighed heavily on his mind in the opening months. Even so he took his goal well, and with Iwelumo doubtful for the Christmas games and Todorov out long term, he would surely have a part to play in the second half of the season.

The festive period could be pivotal in our season, and judging by the four fixtures, they all looked winnable. Luckily we were not playing any teams in the top half, so there were points up for grabs. Four points off top spot could easily be made up, and home games against two sides with poor away form meant by 2 January our home form could match our impressive away record we hoped.

It seemed as though we would have to dig out a result against at home to Hull with all our injuries. Chris Dickson had returned from Gillingham after eleven in fourteen and would maybe make his home bow against Hull. Dickson started on the bench, which was no surprise, but it was to see McLeod there. After his first goal, surely he'd have been full of confidence, and with Zheng and Big Chris less than fully fit, the game would have been a great opportunity for him to score again.

Hull were mid table but impressed in the first half. Frazier Campbell put them in front with a fine finish, showing his Manchester United class. But the first half ended on a sour note with a nasty scuffle involving Danny Mills and our ex-player Bryan Hughes. From where I was, it seemed as though Hughes lashed out at Mills and should have been shown a straight red. For once Mills actually did little wrong and was the victim.

In the second half despite an equaliser from Bougherra, our injuries took their toll as we had some players who were not 100 per cent fit and again had a defender sent off. Danny Mills lived up to his reputation. After being booked for dissent, he then talked himself into a red card. Mills had been excellent since arriving on loan and looked like staying after his loan but had let the side down massively. Tensions were high after the first half scuffle, and Mills needed to calm down. The referee maybe did not have the best game; however, the sending off was all Mills' fault.

It is wrong to accuse Mills of being unprofessional and deliberately getting himself red-carded to get Christmas off. However, nothing in football is surprising, and he would not have been the first footballer to get a dubious card around the festive period. This does not change the fact that his card could have cost us three points and a valuable defender for some vital games. Also, Mills had been a liability at times in his discipline; against Norwich he was lucky not to be sent off. If he could have cut out this side of his game and let his ability speak for itself, maybe he would have had more England caps and earned a permanent move to the Valley.

Luckily our depleted team held out for a draw, but for Weaver in the last minute it could have been worse. There was a major positive though: the return of Paddy McCarthy for his first game since September after Sodje was taken off injured. McCarthy did not have the best of starts at the club. Maybe this was related to an injury he had at Leicester before signing, but he slotted in well against Hull and would be needed in the coming weeks.

Pardew came out and publically criticised Mills. To be fair to Pardew he had every right after Mills' stupidity. This seemed to be the end of Mills' Charlton career as he would now be suspended for the remaining games of his loan and may have blown his chances. With Yassin injured as well, we would need reinforcements in the transfer window, albeit probably on loan.

The only positive that I could see out of Reid's injury was that as he would be out till after the window, maybe no team would want to sign an injured player. Also, despite his obvious quality, his injury jinx had struck again. With Todorov out there would also be the chance we would bring in one or two players to strengthen the squad.

As always at Christmas the games were plenty. We had two away games in a matter of days at Norwich and Leicester. After comfortably beating them both at home, there was hope of similar results. Neither side was challenging us for promotion, and with our good away record and the need for a healthy return from the festive period, we had to fancy our chances.

As it turned out the two 1–1 draws seemed more like points gained than two lost. At Norwich we gave away the lead but played a large majority of the game with ten men after Sodje was sent off for a two-footed lunge. We could have no complaints as it was a certain red, but discipline was becoming an issue. With a lot of injuries even more cards were not helping matters. But managing to get a result with ten men again was pleasing as again we had shown spirit and determination.

This show of character was seen again in the draw at Leicester. After falling behind late on, we scored an injury-time leveller through McCarthy. Not the best performance, but we'd kept eleven on the pitch, and with bottom side Colchester up next, it might not be such a bad Christmas. Pardew praised the team after Leicester, and luckily we had not lost too much ground at the top. Watford were struggling after an excellent start, and no team was consistent enough to take advantage of other teams' slips.

On the same day we drew at Leicester, across London at West Ham, Alan Curbishley's West Ham continued their fine run against Manchester United with a 2–1 win. So far this season West Ham had been a bit like the

Charlton of old; they were ninth in the top flight with European ambitions. The only difference was that Curbs now had far more money at his disposal. Apparently some fans at West Ham were not best pleased with Curbishley's brand of football and the fact they were no higher in the league. This was ridiculous as West Ham had survived by the skin of their teeth the season before and now were more than comfortable in mid table. The football they played may not have been like Brazil's, but it was not Bolton. He had spent a fair bit on players such as Bellamy and Parker, but had some bad injury problems, including Kieron Dyer breaking his leg, as well as the departure of Tevez. To think people called Charlton fans fickle.

While West Ham had just beaten the champions of Europe-elect we were playing Colchester at home on New Year's Day. As it turned out this was one of the lowest points of the season. The performance all round was poor, and even though Colchester played well, there is no way we should have lost. Kevin Lisbie got a good reception on his return and showed us what we were missing with two goals. The second was a fine overhead kick, but the defending was awful. It was evident we were massively missing a player such as Reid or Todorov as there was no creativity and a clear lack of quality in midfield. Luke Varney pulled a goal back, but as in the Burnley game we didn't sufficiently build on this and rightly in my opinion the team were booed off at the end. Even though booing your team during a game has detrimental effects and is arguably not right, fans do pay a lot of money to follow their team; so when the whistle goes at the end, they should exercise their right to make their feelings known.

The team let the fans down this day and doubts began about whether the squad had enough to gain promotion. It was far too early to question Pardew's role, but our home form was a worry, and some of the performances particularly against the bottom sides had been dire. Looking at the table we were still fifth, which was relatively healthy, but we needed a more consistent 2008.

The cup game against West Brom on the following Saturday would be a welcome break from the league and a chance for one or two of the fringe players to stake a claim. One player who would play was Kelly Youga, a left back who actually signed for the club under Curbishley but had been on loan a number of times and was only now set to debut. With Basey and Thatcher injured and Powell in need of a rest, there was need for freshening up at the back. Youga was a fiery character after being sent off twice already this season.

Against West Brom we played a lot better and deserved the win but found our old keeper Dean Kiely in good form. A draw was not particularly great as it meant a replay, but the performance was a lot better overall. Youga played well at left back to suggest he would play more whilst Dickson came on as a sub and almost won the game.

After feeling very low after the Colchester game, suddenly there were reasons to feel positive again. We had two players back from loans who would improve the squad whilst the transfer window was now open.

Our next game against Blackpool was almost the opposite of the Colchester game. We played some terrific football, and our 4–1 victory could have been a lot more but for their keeper. Kelly Youga making his league debut gave an excellent performance at left back. He looked sold defensively but also treated the fans to some step overs, showing that going forward he can offer a threat.

Luke Varney and Izale McLeod started up front and looked – just as Varney and Iwelumo had earlier in the season – as though they could form a fine partnership. The Blackpool defence could not live with their pace. Varney scored a good goal whilst McLeod was unlucky not to get on the score sheet and deservedly left the pitch to a standing ovation. Iwelumo had been excellent, but without him in the side there was less lumping the ball forward whenever options were limited. Pardew's ball-playing philosophy really worked against Blackpool, and yet again there was optimism.

We then faced a cup replay against West Brom. Unfortunately after fighting back from 2–0 down, we lost on penalties No tears shed here though with some big games ahead. Chris Dickson had come on as a substitute to score the equaliser further enhancing his reputation as a terrific finisher, so it was still a positive night.

On the Friday before a vital away game at Watford, it was announced we had signed Andy Gray from Burnley, initially on loan so he could play on the Saturday, but the following week he would sign for £1.5 million. Even though he had played well against us in December and had an impressive scoring record in the Championship, £1.5 million is a lot for a thirty-year-old who had not impressed when playing in the Premiership. I felt that £1.5 million was a lot of money for us when there were other younger strikers out there and players that were more likely to be regulars if we got promoted.

Alan Pardew talked about Gray's goal scoring ability in the Championship as well as the quality and link-up play we had been missing recently. The hope was that Gray would prove his doubters wrong. Certainly his record for mid table Burnley was good enough to suggest he would get near to one in two for us.

The Watford game was on Sky Sports and was another opportunity to see us against another promotion contender. We turned in another terrific performance and deserved to win but struggled to finish. One lapse at the back cost us, but after Ambrose scored a lucky goal, both substitutes Gray and Dickson had chance to win it. After coming from behind, there were mixed feelings about not winning, but a point away at Watford was a good result. Because we'd played the rest of the top six away and they still had to come to the Valley meant that promotion felt as though it was still there for the taking.

Watford would be challenging near the top, but they had been dealt a blow after Marlon King left for Wigan. He had scored plenty for Watford, so surely they would struggle a bit more now. Near the top though West Brom spent big on striker Luke Moore, as did Wolves with Ebanks-Blake, so we were not the only ones to strengthen.

Our good run continued against Stoke, who themselves were in the promotion picture. After playing very well and creating a fair few chances, our side faced another draw, but Lloyd Sam gave us a priceless win with less than ten minutes to go. Andy Gray made his full debut and impressed despite not scoring whilst Nicky Weaver made a terrific last minute save to ensure the win.

Suddenly we were back in the running, and only four points off top spot in late January was very healthy.

The Stoke game was another highlight in the season, at their place they had effectively bullied us to win the game. But in the reverse fixture, Charlton played excellently at times and showed as a team they had adpated very well to the physical demands of the second tier and a passing game could reap rewards. The game itself was another fine advert for the Championship as the two conflicting styles were on show.

Two days after though we were dealt the biggest blow since relegation when Andy Reid was sold to Sunderland. Even though £4 million was good money for Charlton in the days of inflated prices, it felt as though we could have got more for a player of his talent. This was not the only reason why his sale angered Charlton fans. Reid had pledged his future to the club earlier in the season, and the feeling was that surely we could have persuaded him to stay as unlike other players he had never publically stated any desire to leave.

With Charlton sitting pretty in the table, Reid would have had a big part to play, and if we failed to get promotion, he could have left at the end of the season for similar money. I know a lot of fans felt let down by the board in sanctioning the move. We were not in such a bad situation that we had to accept Sunderland's offer, and there is no way his value would have changed drastically between January and May. Also, even though we had begun to cope well without Reid since the Colchester game, he would still be missed greatly, and a few good performances did not cover up how big a loss he would be.

The sale replicated the sale of Scott Parker four years previously. Some fans believe that when Parker was sold that started our decline as it virtually ended our European ambitions and meant we could not go to that next level. Scott Parker was a quality player capable of playing for a top-four club and England, so he was not going to stay forever. But if we'd kept him and been a bit braver in turning down £10 million, who knows what we'd have achieved? Danny Murphy did a good job replacing Parker, and likewise his departure was hard to take, but with Reid leaving and no clear replacement, this was possibly our biggest loss. Now that we were in the Championship it would be even harder to attract the kind of player who added anywhere near Reid's quality and value to the team. At least when we were in the top flight, finding someone to replace the sales was easier.

Alan Pardew was not too heavily criticised for Reid's sale, but he said something that seemed ridiculous when he said he hoped selling Reid would make us stronger. There was no way selling our star man could possibly make us stronger. Four million pounds is a lot to any Championship club; however, with the window shutting on the day Reid left, there was no opportunity to spend the money, and our promotion hopes had been massively hit.

We signed two players on loan: Greg Halford from Sunderland and Lee Cook from Fulham. These seemed like excellent loans. Halford had done very well at Colchester, but his career stalled at Sunderland. Cook had looked an excellent player at QPR before injuries stopped him making an impression in the top flight. Cook certainly seemed to have similar attributes to Reid, so if he could get properly fit, maybe Reid's loss would not be such a big deal.

In the aftermath of the Stoke game, we also lost Dickson for the rest of the season after a freak accident in a hotel lobby. This was not as big a blow as the loss of Reid was, but after making quite an impression in recent weeks, Dickson could have helped in the goal scoring department. Iwelumo was our only striker who looked like reaching double figures.

After some excellent performances, we had a massive disappointment losing at twenty-third place Scunthorpe. Even though we came up against another good goalkeeper, the performance was nowhere near good enough. Mouts made an error for the winning goal, which would cost him his place, but in all honesty we were not ruthless in front of goal. It was the kind of game where – dare I say it – Andy Reid could have proved the difference.

Luckily our next game was the perfect chance for us to put the Scunthorpe game behind us, at home to Neil Warnock's Palace – we were fifth, Palace seventh – so it was a massive match. This was the first Friday-night match I had been to for years after police advice following crown trouble at Selhurst. Charlton fans have no reputation for causing trouble, and after a number of Palace fans were convicted of violence following the match of 1 September, there was an extra police presence at the game.

This was the first time Palace had visited the Valley since we sent them down. As we had only played them a few times since the start of the century, the rivalry is hardly the fiercest in the country. But on a Friday night under the lights, it would have the same feel as a north London or Tyne–Wear derby.

Crystal Palace at home had actually been my first Charlton match as a season-ticket holder. After getting a half-season ticket in 1999, the Boxing Day game would be the first game of hundreds sitting in the east stand as a regular. We won 2–1 that day. It proved to be the start of a record number of wins for the club, which culminated in our winning the league. A repeat would be very nice.

We put in another excellent home performance. The 2–0 win was massive, and Luke Varney showed us his undoubted quality with two very well-taken goals. It could have been a couple more, and for the third home game in a row, I left the ground feeling very optimistic. Doing the double over your local rivals always puts gloss on a season, no matter where you finish. But after beating another side near the top, we felt very positive.

Luke Varney had admitted that he had struggled to adapt to the Championship and the pressures of Charlton. The transfer fee was a lot – and injury at the start did not help – but he had shown in parts what a quality player we had. Against Palace his two goals were superb finishes, and if he could play like that more often, we'd have someone challenging for near to twenty goals a season.

The following Tuesday we played away at Sheffield Wednesday in what proved to be a decent 0–0 draw. Nicky Weaver was first class in goal, and one save from Bullen was particularly good, so it felt like a point gained. We remained in fifth place, where we'd remained pretty much since early December. Weaver may not be the fans' favourite, but at times he had saved us just as much as the keepers he had to follow in Kiely and Carson.

After the game Pardew talked of our lack of away numbers. Even though Sheffield on a Tuesday is long way and inconvenient for a lot of fans, throughout the season our away following had been comparatively poor. For a team that gets more than 20,000 for every home game to take only a few hundred to most away games is unimpressive, especially when you see sides such as Bristol City bringing around 2,000 to the Valley. I think the club should do more to encourage fans to follow Charlton away. When we subsidised prices for Ewood Park in 2007, it worked a treat. I know Charlton cannot afford to do this every week, but a possible solution would be to award loyalty points for away games, and when you achieve a certain amount, ticket prices are reduced.

Clubs such as Chelsea have a loyalty-point scheme. The reward is centred on earlier availability for more points holders. Unfortunately Charlton do not sell out quickly, so this would not work. But if we reduced prices for more points holders, surely it would attract a higher away following.

Alan Pardew also advocated away fans at the Valley being moved as where they currently sit, the Jimmy Seed stand, has better acoustics than much of the ground. Pardew was right to look into a possibility of housing home fans there, but it is the least developed part of the stadium, so there are a number of reasons why it would not work.

The point is, however, that many away teams tend to fill the away end, and as our performances have not been consistent at home for a long time, they often appear to be louder than the home fans are. If the team could produce on the pitch, the home fans would respond and there would be no need to question the atmosphere from the home fans. Our home fans do create a cracking atmosphere even in times of adversity, so Charlton have much bigger issues to deal with. The club have since decided not to pursue this as it's not practical due to segregation issues, coupled with the fact we struggle to fill the ground, so we would possibly be left with another half-empty stand.

After a well-earned draw at Wednesday, we drew again at home to Watford. Before the game looking at the table, it was another massive game. They were top. A win would close the gap to four points. It seemed as though Watford were not suffering from the loss of King, and we knew the game would be one of our hardest.

At half-time we were deservedly 2–0 up. Ambrose scored again against Watford. The front two in Varney and Gray had linked up well despite not scoring themselves. Typically though a crazy three minutes in the second half meant we blew it. A score of 2–2 was not the worst result as automatic promotion was still in reach, but obviously a win would have been such as boost. Also at 2–2 we could have caved in and lost it, but a draw against possibly the best side in the league over the first thirty-odd games was still OK.

I blame Paul Merson for the away side's turnaround. Even though I was at the game, on *Soccer Saturday* he was doing the report and on more than one occasion said that there was no way Watford would score and get back into the game. Talk about tempting fate as after equalising Watford could easily have gone on to win the game.

We knew that there was a need for more consistency if we were to get automatic promotion, but we could not put two results together. Our constant Jekyll-and-Hyde form continued with two away games against Blackpool in lower mid table and then Sheffield United with outside playoff ambitions.

Before the Blackpool game I watched the Birmingham–Arsenal match on Sky. The match will now always be remembered for Eduardo's horrific injury. Even watching the match on television, to me it was sickening. How the players could get back into the game afterwards is beyond me. Amazingly though Eduardo eventually returned, and judging by a couple of the goals he has scored since, he will be back to his best by 2009–0.

Watching *Soccer Saturday*, I thought our game seemed like a thriller. It summed up our season as we fell 2–0 down, fought back well to 2–2 and then conceded three more in ten minutes to kill the game. A 5–3 defeat was hugely disappointing. To concede so many is outrageous and looked like all but ending our automatic hopes. Greg Halford had a poor game at the back, but he was not the only one. If our season had not been so inconsistent in terms of performances, this could have been written off as a freak result. This sort of result had been on the cards, and it was not the first time the defence had played so badly.

Only a few weeks before we had destroyed Blackpool. Now they had given us a real thrashing. Blackpool would stay up, but were an average side; they had some good players but should never have scored five goals against us. After Pardew talked of the importance of away support, at Bloomfield Road we took a healthy following, but they were incredibly let down.

During the week we signed Scott Sinclair on loan from Chelsea, which seemed an excellent move. He had done well on loan at other Championship clubs and has blistering pace so would add an extra dimension to our midfield.

Remarkably though we then went and won comfortably with a superb performance away at Sheffield United. Iwelumo scored his first in ages, and we stifled the threat of Beattie really well. Alan Pardew rightly praised the side and admitted we still had a sniff of automatic promotion. It would be difficult, but a first away win since early December and a terrific performance banished the memories of Blackpool.

Many pundits had criticised the lack of quality in the Championship. Having seen almost every side either at the Valley or on TV, I think that was somewhat unfair. The Championship was the most competitive of all the leagues in England, and it is no exaggeration to say anyone could beat anyone else. Alan Pardew, when discussing this, talked of the higher quality in the lower half of the league, and he was right. Teams such as Colchester although near the bottom still had some quality players (Lisbie and Sheringham, for example).

Teams expected to do well had struggled, Sheffield United being the prime example, whilst some other teams, including Hull and our next opponents Bristol City, were doing exceptionally well and were top going into the game. Throughout the season we tended to do better against the top sides and struggle against the bottom, so hopes were that this would continue against

Bristol City. Obviously I can only speculate to the reasons why we played better against the sides nearer the top, but certainly at the Valley it appeared we struggled with the pressure of the levels of expectation.

The Bristol City game was on a Tuesday under the lights, so the atmosphere was sure to be electric. City brought a lot of fans to the game who generated a lot of noise in what turned out to be a real game of two halves, certainly according to Pardew. As in the Watford game, we were seven points off the automatic promotion spots, so a win would significantly close the gap.

During the first half we played very well, Ambrose scoring again. But yet again we could not hold on and in the second half were outplayed. A 1–1 draw was not a bad result as City showed that they could play good football as well as bags of spirit. At the end it was bit end to end, but when City scored it had been coming and was no surprise. Their fans as well were top drawer. All night they got behind their side and created a lot of noise, despite one fan throwing a flare onto the pitch.

Sinclair made his home bow, and to say he unimpressed is an understatement. He got into a couple of good positions but wasted them by trying too many tricks and not getting his head up. It may seem unfair to criticise a player who was making a fourteen-minute debut, but when you are desperate for a win and you have a talented player with the ball in promising positions, it is hard not to get annoyed.

The day after there was another exciting loan signing arriving in Leroy Lita. With Dickson out for the season and the other forwards struggling for consistency, our front line needed freshening up. McLeod had gone on loan to Colchester, but then got a season-ending injury after a challenge by Plymouth's Timar (again), so Lita was a welcome addition.

Lita had struggled this season for Reading in the top flight but had done very well the season before and had a very good scoring record in the Championship, including when he helped fire Reading to the title in 2006. Andy Gray was yet to get off the mark, and the goals for Iwelumo and Varney had significantly dried up so we hoped Lita could at least help us to a playoff place.

If we didn't already know, our next three games made automatic promotion impossible and even casted doubt over the playoffs. For the second time we lost three on the bounce, and there was little to take from any of the games.

At home to relegation-threatened Preston, we were awful all round, and this mirrored the Colchester home game. They could have been at least two up at half-time, but Weaver kept us in the game. Even when we scored with fifteen minutes to go and looked like getting an underserved point, some further poor defending led to Preston winning the game. For the first time since Colchester, the team was rightly booed off, and as Alan Pardew rightly said, the players didn't do justice to the quality and character we obviously have. Since Pardew became boss, his communication with the fans always seemed quite good. To say that he would have booed some of our play was at least something good to hear.

About our next two away games, the less said the better: two away defeats without even scoring at Burnley and then Ipswich. In both games our performances were not as bad as it had been at Preston and the goals scored against us were special, but again we struggled to score goals and were in a bad run at exactly the wrong time. A player like Reid or Todorov could have made such a difference in these types of games

The Ipswich game left us tenth in the league, our lowest position since August, and we had some difficult fixtures ahead. What made things worse was that at the very top, no one else could find the necessary consistency. Five points separated the top five, so automatic promotion had slipped through our fingers after no team really standing out or running away with it.

West Brom were in the top five, and with their quality looked a real good bet for the top two. So with their visiting the Valley after three consecutive defeats, even the playoffs were starting to look a big ask. Alan Pardew's programme column made interesting reading as he admitted responsibility for putting our playoff hopes in jeopardy. This was fair as he had to take a share of the blame. The results had not been good enough, and many of the signings (loan and permanent) had not worked out.

Against West Brom we more than matched the best footballing side in the division, and for the fourth game against them the result could have gone either way, but a 1–1 draw seemed fair. Walking away from the ground, fans were frustrated because the playoffs seemed a long way off, yet we had proved against the top sides we were good enough. Pardew said he felt the playoffs were not impossible, but with games running out and since we had not won back-to-back games since December, serious doubt was cast over this.

In the week between home games, Scott Sinclair returned to Chelsea before joining Palace on loan. He had made no impression since signing and would not be missed. Disappointingly he was not the only loan signing who had failed to live up to his name.

Our next match against Wolves all but sealed our fate after a heartbreaking end. Going into the match against Wolves, we were separated by only a point. The loser would almost certainly be out of the picture. With a matter of minutes to go, we were 2–1 down and chasing the game. Ebanks-Blake had scored one of the goals of the season after turning McCarthy before firing into the top corner. However, Leroy Lita got his head on a long ball into the box and levelled the score. With a few minutes of injury time, we decided to go for the win and threw bodies forward.

Wolves broke away and with the last kick won the game. In that three minutes I think the Charlton fans in the ground went through all the emotions fans go through in a whole season. Before the equaliser I was cursing the fact we would have another season in the Championship, but then when we scored, everything seemed great again, and Charlton were fantastic. Walking away from the Valley, we were gutted. It didn't match Fulham 2006, but now with another season in the second tier, it was questionable whether we'd ever return.

On the Monday cause for optimism for the following season came from sources unlikely sources. I was in a pub with some friends. Standing by the bar were three of our players. Paddy McCarthy was gutted about the way Ebanks-Blake had turned him for one of Wolves' goals but was still upbeat and willing to have a chat. Andy Gray was slightly quieter, maybe because he had not found top form since signing in January. Even though they'd had a few to drink, they seemed intent that next season with the younger players more experienced and the new signings fully settled in we'd be stronger and better.

The third player in the pub, Nicky Weaver, had an eventful three minutes on the pitch against Plymouth in our next game. He was sent off for a deliberate handball and left us with a really difficult task. Nevertheless, the remarkable fact that we'd not lost all season with ten men continued, and two late goals from Leroy Lita again gave us an extraordinary win. The playoffs still were a long way away, but having seemingly got the difficult games out of the way, the Plymouth performance maintained the glimmer.

Robert Elliot had come on for his debut following Weavers red and did well in goal, including making an excellent last-minute save to preserve the points. Elliot was a Charlton fan and had come up through the ranks as many of our current squad had, so it was fantastic to see him play well. This left Pardew with a dilemma: who to play in goal in our next game. Darren Randolph had returned from a successful loan spell and was slightly more experienced, but following Elliot's superb debut, I thought he would get the nod.

Against Southampton I sat in the director's box; this was a new and fascinating experience. I am sure most of the directors as well as the fans were surprised that Elliot did not play after his Plymouth heroics. This decision by Pardew arguably backfired when Randolph made an error for Southampton's goal. Randolph had done a good job at Bury but looked shaky all game, and with Elliot full of confidence, it must have been a massive kick in the teeth for him not to have got the nod.

At half-time we were a goal down. In the hospitality suite I overheard Sir Trevor Brooking say that our midfield was ineffective. Zheng Zhi had been superb all season, but his performances had faded understandably. Playing forty-six games in England is a lot more challenging than playing in the Chinese leagues. It would have been a massive task for him to maintain his early-season form. At home to Southampton, he struggled on the right of midfield but was not the only player to be below par. Lee Cook was not fully fit and did not have anywhere near the same influence as Reid had had.

In the second half Andy Gray scored his first goal for the club; in fact it was his first since scoring against Charlton for Burnley and ended a long drought. This was too late though. If he'd played as well as he had for Burnley, Charlton would certainly have been in the playoffs. Late on we had chances to win it although I doubt we deserved a win.

Sitting in the director's box was completely different from my usual seat, situated in the west stand, which is not renowned for atmosphere. One fan was particularly vocal in his disapproval of the game, the season and the management. In clear ear shot of the board, this fan protested for a change in the summer. On this occasion he was the only one, but I could understand his frustrations as we had massively underachieved.

Away at QPR in the next game, we lost to make it mathematically impossible for us to get into the playoffs. The performance all round was sub-standard, and our season was all but over. After the game Lita and Cook returned to their parent clubs. Lita was required to help Reading try to avoid relegation, and there was no point keeping Cook, who had not been fit enough to cement a regular spot.

If Lita had arrived earlier, he could have made a real difference. His goals against Wolves and Plymouth showed he had the necessary quality, and if he had played more, he could have made up for the other strikers being inept.

Ultimately the signings had not worked out, and the lack of consistency, especially at home, had cost us dearly. Our record against the top sides was as good as West Brom's, who won the league, yet too many times we lost to teams near or at the bottom. Some of the players brought in took far too long to settle whilst some never adapted. Luke Varney and McCarthy looked the part in some games, but initially found it tough whilst Izale McLeod and Gray looked like money not very well spent.

Being in the Championship means that you need loan players to strengthen a squad. The ones we had brought in – with one or two exceptions – did not work out. Danny Mills let himself down against Hull after an excellent first half to the season whilst players such as Halford were too inconstant in their performances.

Even though Pardew has to take a lot of the blame, the board undermined him with the sale of Reid. On many occasions the team was clearly good enough, but the players let the boss down. It was certain to be another busy summer.

Chapter 9

A Smaller, Better Squad

After the QPR game dashed our chances of the playoffs, we still had two games to play. These games in terms of the table were insignificant for us, but two players made quite an impression in their first and last appearances for the club.

Jonjo Shelvey was another product of our academy and at sixteen became Charlton's youngest player away at Barnsley. Even though we got beaten comfortably, he stood out as being a real prospect with a composed performance in midfield. He would also play in our final game at home to Coventry and would enhance the fans' hopes for the following season.

Shelvey was excellent against Coventry but was overshadowed by Chris Powell, who made his final appearance for Charlton. Powell was to be released as we could not afford to keep him at the club, and he wanted to continue playing. Pardew apparently wanted to keep him; but the decision was out of his hands, so he would leave. Powell will quite probably make a fine coach, and

Pardew saw this potential; but finances stopped this happening at Charlton.

We had nothing but pride to play for against Coventry. They were in slight danger of relegation, Iain Dowie had been sacked after a fallout with their board and his replacement Chris Coleman had not yet ensured their safety. Obviously as a Charlton fan, I was quite pleased to see Dowie struggle to make a managerial impression after his spell with us.

After eighty-odd minutes we were 3–1 up and had played well. Shelvey looked a lot older physically and in the way he controlled the midfield. Someone so young to look so composed on the ball with a fine range of passing was excellent to see. Varney and Gray scored a couple of cracking goals to suggest they would be a lot better next season. Scott Wagstaff also made his home debut to suggest he may push Lloyd Sam next season.

Chris Powell came on for a cameo in an unfamiliar midfield role As someone who had scored only two Charlton goals in more than 250 games, it seemed too much like a fairytale ending for him to get a goal, unless of course we got a penalty. The goals he had scored had also both been against Powell's beloved Spurs, but thosewere a long time ago.

Amazingly very late on, he made a darting run into the box and bundled the ball in to end his Charlton career on the perfect note. I think that Powell had been wasted at left back as with his cultured left foot and new-found eye for the goal, he could have been a superb midfielder. The other players showed their appreciation for such a legend by lifting him up after scoring, and the lap of honour was all about Powell. Even though every Charlton fan was sorry to see him leave, there is always the possibility he will one day return as a player, coach or even manager.

At least the season had ended on a high. Alan Pardew said after the game that we had a real gem in Shelvey; coupled with other young players the future was very bright. A few players also made positive sounds about the coming season, including Andy Gray, who had been a one in two goals to games man before joining us, so there was no doubt in his ability. If we learnt anything from 2007–8, it was we cannot learn too much from one performance. Against Coventry the front two excelled up front and Gray led the line very well.

A couple of weeks after our season ended, I went to the playoff final between Hull and Bristol City. Obviously I was hugely disappointed Charlton were not there, but to be at the game was still a great experience. Crystal Palace under Warnock nearly made the final but fell short. despite my obvious dislike for Palace, Warnock did a fine job at Selhurst, and they'd surely be stronger next season, especially as like ourselves they had some promising young players.

The most expensive game of the season with £30 million at stake was not the best game of football I had ever seen, but the atmosphere was tremendous and the goal to win the game was quality from Dean Windass. One noticeable thing about the two sides was that on paper the squads did not have the same quality as Charlton had. Of course we deserved to finish eleventh and not go up. But when questioning how many of their players would get into a Charlton side and vice versa, there was more quality in our team with the exception of Frazier Campbell and Michael Turner. I could not see Hull – or Stoke, who surprisingly got promotion – staying in the Premiership. They had some good players; but the step up is massive, and their star man, Campbell, would possibly return to United.

I doubted if there would be a management change at Charlton; but in football you never know. Alan Pardew struggled a little in his first season at West Ham to get them promoted, and they lost to Palace in the playoffs; but in his second they went up, so obviously the hope was that this would again be the case. The squad in the last season was perhaps too big as there was never anything like a consistent side. Forty players are far too many. If we could limit the number, the season should be more fruitful.

Due to the finances following failing to bounce back, there would be no spending spree; there would, however, be plenty of business. The loan signings returned to their clubs whilst a number of players also left. Ben Thatcher joined Powell in leaving on a free after struggling with injuries in 2007–8. Additionally, with Youga and Basey having impressed at left back and having signed new deals, neither Powell nor Thatcher would be regulars.

Disappointingly we lost three of the better performers from the previous season, two of which to fellow contenders for promotion in 2009.

First, Paddy McCarthy went to Palace, which was a blow. After a shaky start, he had been one of the better performers in the second half of the season. Even though he could not be guaranteed a regular spot, Paddy would certainly have provided excellent competition and would be more than an able deputy if required.

When The Robin Stopped Bobbing

Another reason McCarthy would be missed was the loss of Madjid Bougherra. If Bougherra stayed, he'd maybe have been first choice ahead of Paddy. To lose both left us short at the back. You could not begrudge Bougherra the move though. He signed for Rangers who were in the Champions League. Bougherra had been injured for parts of the season, but we had defended a lot better with him in the side. Our good run at the start of the season had Madjid and Fortune in central defence whilst our good run in January included Madjid and McCarthy.

The third and possibly the biggest loss was Iwelumo, who left for Wolves. He had been superb in the first half of the season. Unfortunately in the second he, – like the rest of the team – lost some form and was used in the wrong way. Iwelumo was too often used just as a target man when, as shown by some of his early goals, Big Chris is pretty handy on the floor and scores a few with his right foot. Players such as him and Gray are best utilised when you get balls into the box for them to attack or give them the ball on the edge of the box so they can link the play or turn their man, certainly not when the ball is lumped forward aimlessly. A major disappointment surrounded the fee, for a player who had proved himself in the second tier, the money he left for was peanuts compared to some of the money spent on strikers in the Championship (I include our own signings in this).

All three players would go on to have superb seasons. Bougherra won player of the year as Rangers won a league and cup double. Iwelumo was on fire at the start as he helped Wolves to the Championship title. McCarthy also showed the Palace fans what he had shown us the year before.

What made these losses even worse was the lack of substantial fees for the three. We received £2.5 million for Bougherra; but this was the same price we paid, and it was a massive disappointment to lose possibly our best defender for an amount that didn't reflect his quality. As with the Reid loss, we had got decent money but felt it could and should have been more.

We would also lose Jerome Thomas, Marcus Bent and Amady Faye. The latter two had been on loan so no surprise or tears shed there, but Thomas would be missed despite sometimes being quite a frustrating player. Thomas went to Portsmouth, where injuries hampered him. We missed his skills and trickery on the left. Again there were no real substantial fees for these players, which were disappointing certainly since we shelled out more than £4.5 million on them.

As for the players we brought in, there was nothing like the number seen in 2007; we tried for quality over quantity. Mark Hudson certainly looked like a quality player and a fantastic bit of business as he signed on a free after leaving Palace. Hudson was very highly rated and had been linked with a Premiership move; he was a bit of a coup for the club.

Hudson received the armband, which seemed a wise choice as he had done exceptionally well at Palace in the role. Pardew talked of his leadership qualities, which would prove vital as since Reid left, we perhaps lacked inspirational characters.

Nicky Bailey also looked a decent signing; he had done very well in League One for Southend and looked more than capable of the step up. Our midfield had struggled towards the end of the season, so it was hoped

Bailey could add some quality and goals. For less than a million, again, it looked as though we had spent well.

Our third and final permanent signing was Stuart Fleetwood, who'd scored bundles in the Blue Square Premier for Forest Green. At only twenty-two he had plenty of potential; a tribunal would decided the fee, but it would not be substantial. As with Chris Dickson there was no guarantee he would play regularly but would maybe go on loan and hopefully come back and challenge Varney and Gray, who looked as though they'd be first choice. Fleetwood had bags of pace so could also be effectively used as a sub.

Alan Pardew talked of the unsuccessful loan signings from the season before and the need to avoid this happening again. The loans he went for appeared as though they'd make more of a positive impact. All three were fit, needed regular football and had Premiership experience. Martin Cranie and Linvoy Primus came on loan from Portsmouth to strengthen the defence whilst Hameur Bouazza joined from Fulham for the year to help replace the departing Thomas. Even though they'd not played much the previous season, it was evident they were coming to play football, unlike the loans last season who needed to get their fitness up and would definitely return to their parent clubs.

When loan signings join a club, there is always a question over their desire to play and do well for the club. Quite often they just want to put themselves in the shop window. However, Bouazza would join for the season, so he was like a permanent player and would maybe sign a deal at the end. Cranie and Primus were also here long term and would unlikely go back to Portsmouth and be regulars, so there was the possibility they'd stay longer than their loans.

Our squad was smaller than last season's squad, and due to the losses we were understandably not amongst the favourites for promotion. After the previous season when the pressure got to the players certainly at home, not having the same weight of expectation would surely help us, and we still looked like a decent bet for the playoffs. When reading through the sports sections and pull-outs, I saw that many pundits were still tipping us for a better finish this time around. The worst case scenario would be a repeat of the end of last season.

The preseason games had gone well. Andy Gray especially got a few goals. Fleetwood and Dickson also got on the score sheet. After not finding a settled front two and too many strikers struggling for confidence, we needed to ensure this did not happen again. Varney got eight league goals; with any luck he'd be pushing for nearer to fifteen. Gray likewise. Up front Todorov was near fitness and after a good start the previous season, surely would help provide the much-needed quality and link-up play we'd missed.

In our final preseason game at home to Athletic Club from Spain, we lost but more than matched our Spanish counterparts. Rob Elliot made two excellent saves to show again he would be an able deputy if called upon whilst Shelvey also looked as if he would play more in 2008–9. Shelvey received the number 7 jersey. Although not having the same tradition as at United or Liverpool, it implied Shelvey was seen as more than a bit-part player.

Kelly Youga in the first half had a poor game. Pardew criticised him after the game for his performance. This had been coming for a while. He came back from his loan in January and looked very dependable, but it did not take long for his performances to dip and his weaknesses to show. You have to question our coaches as unexplainably he seemed to have gone backwards. As Dickson had done, Youga had done outstandingly on loan and looked ready for the Championship but had not replicated the loan form. Since he had received squad number 3, Youga would start the season at left back, ahead of Basey.

In the second half against Athletic Club, Amady Faye made his Valley return. No one had yet come in for him. And it looked as though he could remain our player. In the few minutes he was on the pitch, all the memories of the Premiership came flooding back as he looked awful. Pardew said afterwards if he stayed, we'd make best use of him. Fortunately that week Stoke signed him, and he has since played some of his best football there.

The season started inconsistently. As during the latter part of 2007–8, we could not put two good results together. At home, however, we started the season well, and on the opening day got an excellent result against Swansea, who like Scunthorpe the year before, had won League One. Swansea played some excellent football and could have got more from the game. Hudson looked very solid at the back and got on the score sheet as did Gray to start his season in the best possible way. Unlike Scunthorpe, Swansea looked like they would cause many teams problems in the second tier.

Our midfield against Swansea was quite inexperienced. This showed at times and possibly helped prompt Pardew to sign Bailey. But we looked solid at the back and to get off to a winning start was very pleasing, especially in a game we'd probably have struggled in the year before.

Our next two games were not quite so impressive. First, lower division Yeovil knocked us out of the Carling Cup, which was no overly disappointing as the team was slightly under strength. Then to lose at Watford and play badly was an early blow. It would have been nice to have beaten Yeovil and then got a Premiership away tie in the next round (spoken like a true lower-division fan), but there were no tears shed.

At Watford Nicky Bailey made his debut and impressed; otherwise, the performance was sub-standard. We lost Kelly Youga to a debatable first half red; but after a great record with ten men the previous year and a great result against Swansea to go away with nothing, was disappointing. To make matters worse, we lost Thierry Racon to a long-term injury. He had not cemented a place the year before, but a loan at Brighton had helped him develop. Having started the season well in midfield, to lose him was further bad news.

As Hull showed the year before, a good start was not always necessary to have a good season. But with some difficult games coming up, the prospect of being stuck in mid table early on did not fill me with optimism.

As many games had in 2007–8, our next game at home to Reading gave the fans real hope of a successful season. Reading had just been relegated from the top flight and were the favourites to bounce back. They'd held onto some of their top players, including Doyle and Hunt, so were odds on to win at the Valley.

Similar to the games against Ipswich and Palace in 2007–8, Charlton turned in a fantastic performance, especially going forward. Although it was an incredibly open game and Reading missed a first-half penalty, we more than matched them, and the 4–2 win reflected our attacking talents. A thoroughly entertaining game ended with six goals, three penalties and a red card. It must have been brilliant to watch on Sky. Being there it seemed as though every time a team went forward there would be a goal. I had a spare ticket for the game and took a friend who's not the biggest football fan. I'm sure even he enjoyed the game, but it took some explaining that this did not happen every week and we were not normally this good.

Luke Varney got off the mark with an excellent header whilst Bouazza scored one of our goals of the season with a cracking volley. Alan Pardew was full of praise for Varney afterwards, who himself came out later that week and talked of the extra responsibility on his shoulders this season as Charlton's main man up front. Against Reading he was involved in three of the goals and caused them all sorts of problems to suggest he would turn in more consistent performances this time around and could improve his goal ratio.

Nicky Bailey made his home debut and excelled in midfield He looked to have all the attributes to be a top midfielder in the Championship. Pardew stated that he and Hudson had improved the spine of our team. Even though there were only three games gone, such a result indicated that maybe this would be a more successful year. Reading caused us plenty of problems to highlight our own defensive weaknesses, but we'd beaten one of the favourites comfortably and went temporarily (for about two hours) top of the table.

Typically we then lost two games on the bounce. The first one was away at Preston, who were now much tougher opposition than they'd been the year before. Nevertheless, we surrendered the lead, and some individuals played below par. Luke Varney was excellent up front but couldn't score. Andy Gray got his third in four games. But at the back silly mistakes cost us the game, particularly from Yassin Moutaouakil, who would lose his place to the new recruit Cranie.

On the day of the Preston away game, just across the River Thames, West Ham thrashed Blackburn to win their second of three matches. Despite their impressive start, Alan Curbishley left the club after less than two years in charge. Curbs resigned, but the reports were that he was effectively forced out after some of their players were sold without his consent. This, along with the fans of West Ham treating him badly, probably left Curbs with little choice but to leave.

In 2007–8 during a West Ham home win against Derby, the fans chanted 'You don't know what you're doing' at Curbishley even though they finished a very respectable tenth. In his last days in charge during a home league cup tie at home to Macclesfield, the fans apparently chanted 'You're gonna get sacked in the morning', which was disgraceful. If West Ham were bottom of the league or in the middle of an awful run, fans' frustrations would have been understandable – as shown by Charlton when we lost to Wycombe and the chants to Les Reed were not too different – but at West Ham the future was looking very bright.

Following Preston there was then the traditional early-season international break. Like Charlton the national side turned in two very different performances. England struggled somewhat away in Andorra but then thrashed the highly rated Croatia to get some revenge for the previous November. Theo Walcott scored a fantastic hat trick to enhance his own reputation and further give the nation hope for the World Cup in 2010. For the first time since the days of Eriksson, the side played like a team, and the quality shone through.

One downside from the two away games was that not as many fans could watch them because of Setanta gaining the rights to England games. It is ridiculous that the public have to pay even more to watch England matches. The BBC or ITV should have full rights rather than making fans pay an additional amount even if they already have Sky or another package. I know fans of cricket are upset Channel 4 no longer broadcasts England games, and this is similar to football. Our national sports should be free for fans to watch.

It is ludicrous that the TV stations battle over live football packages. But with the money generated in the modern game, it is understandable. But with England games there should be no competitions. The BBC tend to provide good coverage of live sport, and since they have lost the rights to show FA Cup matches, there is no longer enough John Motson on the television.

Back to domestic football. Top-of-the-table Wolves turned up at the Valley in good spirits and with two of the league's top goal scorers in Ebanks-Blake and our old player Iwelumo, who'd started the season on fire. Iwelumo would have got a good reception from the home crowd after standing out in an average season for us, but he got injured in the warm-up to give us a big boost before the game.

We would lose 3–1 and deservedly so. We had taken the lead, and I left the ground disappointed. Wolves outplayed us and looked a class apart, but we seemed to cave in once they scored an equaliser. Ironically the match winner on the day in Sam Vokes may not have got onto the pitch had Iwelumo not got injured to compound the misery.

One positive was Nicky Bailey, who scored the opener, one of the goals of the season, a cracking volley from twenty-five yards which flew in the top corner (remember Scholes against Bradford in 2000). If this goal had been scored in the top flight, it would be shown again and again. Bailey had fitted in brilliantly since arriving. It was evident the board had gone a long way to spend the money on him, and so far this seemed justified. Despite the board letting the fans down with some of their decisions over the years, their sanctioning of the Bailey signing should be credited.

After shipping some poor goals in our next two games, the defence was far more solid as two clean sheets were well earned away at Doncaster and then Forest. Both had been promoted, so to have returned without any points would have been immensely frustrating. Away at Doncaster we won 1–0 to win only our second away match of the year with a very solid and disciplined performance. Andy Gray scored again, which was pleasing, but Hudson at the back was almost unbeatable to show that Bailey was not the only new player to make an excellent start.

On a personal level, the Forest away game was overshadowed by my first day at university. A home game would have compromised which day I moved in. Obviously this was all new and exciting, but the day was made slightly better by Charlton getting a well earned 0–0 at Forest. When choosing my university, I would not give up my season ticket, so the University of Kent seemed the perfect choice as it is only an hour's drive from the Valley, which meant I could even make the night games.

The game away at Forest had an element of controversy as they should have been reduced to ten men for denying Varney a goal-scoring opportunity, and we were denied a clear penalty for a handball. Nevertheless, four points and two clean sheets is still commendable, and we looked as though we were getting back to the away form of late 2007.

We lost Jon Fortune to a long-term injury which left us with only two recognised centre halves at the club. Hudson had been excellent, but if he were to get injured or suspended, we'd be in trouble at the back. Primus had joined but was getting on a bit and Hudson is not the most mobile of centre halves, so there was also the worry that strikers would now fancy their chances a little more, especially if they had a bit of pace and decent movement.

Having sold two centre halfs in the summer and Sodje returning to Reading, Pardew had to be questioned about why he did not make the centre half area a priority. We did have Youga and Semedo to cover if needed but neither had great height or experience; anymore long term injuries and we'd be very vulnerable.

During my first week at university, I met many new people and some other football fans. When you are a fan, you tend to meet others, and football is the number one topic of conversation. Some were real football fans from other parts of the country who understood what it's like to truly follow a team, whereas others claimed to follow Manchester United or Chelsea but had no idea who they were playing the following Saturday and thought you were tragic for owning a replica shirt.

The first time I went back home for Charlton was the next Saturday for a game against Sheffield Wednesday. They had an awful away record, so I was cautiously optimistic. In their last away game, Wednesday had been thrashed 6–0 by Reading, and even though they looked on course to be mid table, we had to believe three points were there for the taking.

In the first half we were very dominant and should have been three up. With thirty-five minutes gone, only Varney's strike was the difference, and we paid heavily. Wednesday had two attacks and led at half-time 2–1. With no disrespect to the away side, they were awful but had stolen the lead and spent the whole second half hanging on. We could find no way through. The only positive was the twenty-minute cameo from the returning Todorov. He was off the pace, but it was excellent to see him in a Charlton shirt again.

The game itself will be looked back as a real low point; two bits of bad defending meant we had lost a game that nine times out of ten we'd have won. In the second half, the only thing Weaver had to do was respond to the away fans' chants (Weaver is a massive Wednesday fan). The whole of the away side and their fans must have left the Valley wondering how they had not lost.

I headed back to university angry and disappointed. We had the prospect of our first meeting of the season with Palace the next Tuesday to make up for the Wednesday game. It was also possible that Zheng would return after an injury and that he would make a big difference.

Listening to the radio on the way back, I heard an astonishing result from the Emirates. Hull had beaten Arsenal 2–1 to carry their impressive start to the season. After seeing Hull play at Wembley, I, like most football fans, did not give Hull a prayer of staying up, but they'd surpassed all expectations and played very well at Arsenal. Phil Brown had done well in the market and the players who'd played well in the Championship, including Turner and Myhill, adapted very well. Some of the goals they had scored were special, especially a couple of Geovanni's early efforts.

On the night of the Palace game, I would have preferred to have watched Sky and been kept updated but instead decided to be sociable and sat in a university bar, with no Sky, waiting for my phone to buzz with goal updates. The 1–0 defeat was hard to take, but as I was with new people I tried to hide the disappointment. Unfortunately any Charlton defeat usually hurts badly, and to your local rivals it can be sickening. If my new friends did not know about my obsession, they certainly did now.

When it became clear that yet again we had not played well, there were further calls for a change in management. So far these voices had been minor, but after an indifferent start and some poor results these voices were getting louder. I still though Pardew was the right man. With the quality players coming back to fitness and some seemingly winnable matches coming up, it was too early to call for Pardew's head.

Our start had not been the easiest as we'd played some of the top sides from the previous season (Palace and Watford) as well as the early pace setters. So when looking deeper into our start, it was not disastrous, especially as the playoffs were not a million miles off.

There was a lot of pressure on the Ipswich home game. Luckily for Charlton and Pardew, the players responded, and we fully deserved our 2–1 win, albeit the winner being a lucky own goal. Some players, including Varney, stepped up to the mark in the game. Cranie struggled a little in the first half. His second half replacement, Semedo, looked very accomplished at right back.

Walking away from the ground, I was relieved more than anything. The performance had been good, but it was the result that mattered; and with another international break to go into, the win was greatly needed.

During the break astonishing news broke that Charlton had been interesting investors who'd made an indicative offer for the club, nothing formal yet, but by all accounts the board would recommend the shareholders to accept any offer. These investors were from Zabeel, a Dubai-based investment company, and were apparently billionaires. The potential takeover would make us one of the richest clubs in England. Amazingly it seemed as though if it all went through, with some real cash investment we'd be back in the Premiership sooner rather than later.

In the previous year QPR and Manchester City had been subject to big-money takeovers. This made them hated amongst other football fans. But foreign investment is now a big part of modern-day football, and to be successful, money talks. When it is other teams, as a fan you moan; but when it is your team, you celebrate. To think that we could be one of the richest clubs competing in Europe was phenomenal.

Some Charlton fans understandably did not like the idea of foreign ownership. But in modern-day football, you have to be realistic and accept that even if we got promotion, we'd still need to spend a lot of money to survive. With such a financial difference between the top flight and the Championship, there is no guarantee of long-term survival in the Premiership without cash injections.

I would love Charlton to win the Championship without spending lots of money and to establish ourselves in the top flight similarly to the 2000 promotion when we spent comparatively little (around £8 million) and put a lot of faith in the younger players; but this is not plausible.

Immediately after the high of the news, the reality that nothing had been confirmed in terms of formal offers hit home. The pessimist in me began to think that things were bound to go wrong, and all this hope would disappear. I have to admit though that it was quite enjoyable telling people that Charlton could soon be seriously competing with the likes of Chelsea.

England won both their World Cup qualifiers comfortably, first up against Kazakhstan at Wembley. Lucky enough I was at the game. England eventually got their act together to win the game comfortably. The game was overshadowed somewhat by the booing of Ashley Cole in the second half.

Daniel Macionis

Ashley Cole is not the first England player to be booed by the Wembley crowd. Frank Lampard has said he has become used to it. But I think it is disgraceful that they should have to get used to this. Both players have played consistently well for their country and do not deserve this treatment. They give 100 per cent for England and fully deserve to be in the team. Cole is one of the best left backs in world football whilst Lampard has proved how good he is over the last few years. His scoring record for Chelsea and England is incredible for a midfield player. Cole did make a mistake for the Kazakhstan goal and maybe was not having his best afternoon, but we went onto win the game easily.

Peter Crouch was also booed when playing for England in 2005, yet once he started to get a few goals, he became a hero and one of the crowd's favourites. This shows how fickle fans can be, and I'm sure the same could happen with Cole or Lampard.

This booing is probably more to do with Cole playing for Chelsea and the manner of his transfer from Arsenal than with his actual performance. This of course does not excuse the booing, especially when in previous years players who've played for the equally disliked Manchester United have never had to face such treatment.

I do not like Chelsea but would never boo a player playing for England, even if a Palace player were to turn out for the national side. For the ninety minutes, he is representing his country, not his club, so should be cheered and encouraged if he makes an error. At Wembley the booing of Ashley Cole was quite bad; it certainly seemed to be more than just a minority booing.

When The Robin Stopped Bobbing

Nevertheless, the game was still entertaining, and after Charlton possibly gaining a passport to the elite and having seen England win 5–1, it had been a fantastic few days. Charlton were four points off the top four, and suddenly it looked as though the season could be one of the most exciting in recent history.

Chapter 10

DUBAI PARDEW

After a fantastic international break, all Charlton fans were brought back down to earth on 18 October. Firstly, we received the report that Zabeel were now interested in Premiership Everton, which showed how far we were from any takeover. Then the team lost at Cardiff.

Even though it was only a report, it had also been rumoured Zabeel had looked at West Ham to increase the pessimism. If there was to be a takeover, Alan Pardew must have been sceptical after his relationship with the people in charge at West Ham when they were taken over. His job was already being questioned after an average start. But if we were under new ownership, there would be a fair chance the new owners would want their own man. Part of me believed we needed to win or at least do well in the next few games to show these investors we did not have a bad side. Unfortunately if any were watching at Cardiff, they cannot have been impressed.

We were already a goal down when Jose Semedo got a straight red for denying a goal-scoring opportunity and two goals down when Hudson got his second yellow to kill the game. Fortunately, despite being two goals and two men down, we didn't concede any more as with a fair amount of time to go, it could have been a pasting.

The following Tuesday we had the first of two consecutive home games against Bristol City. Going into the game, we were in eighteenth place, which did not look good, but still only four points off the playoffs. Charlton fans were looking upwards rather than over our shoulders.

After starting really well against Bristol City but not scoring, we made a stupid mistake to gift them an opener and did not recover. In fact the performance was non-existent, and the criticism for the team and Pardew at the end was warranted. Pardew had no complaints about the way the fans reacted but was heavily critical of the team. Nicky Bailey had an unusually bad game. He gave the ball away for their first goal, and we offered little threat going forward after the first half hour.

In the second half when the Charlton fans struggled to find their voice, the away fans' chant of 'You used to be good, but now you're shite' rang out. This was all too true as we had been a really good side, but now we were a side in turmoil. Even when we played Bristol City the previous year, we had in the first half the look of a decent side. The new players we'd signed would have improved the team, but we were missing players such as Iwelumo and Reid.

It is easy to say that you make your own luck, but things were transpiring against us. In the first twenty minutes against City, the team played well, and if we had scored, it could have been different. But Gray hit a post, and Basso made a couple of good saves.

After an exceptionally disappointing game, Conor and I started to question Pardew and considered how a defeat against Burnley could be the end for him. Pardew was right when he questioned whether some members of the side would ever gain the level of consistency needed. He promised a shake up for Saturday, but having lost Zheng for more than three months, there was a question whether this would really make a difference.

Two days before the Burnley match Zabeel pulled out. They stated due to the economic climate, they wanted to concentrate on domestic opportunities. It was still hard to take. In two weeks we'd gone from dreaming of Europe to contemplating another mediocre season. The only consolation was that Zabeel did not invest in another club as this would have been sickening to see what we missed out on.

It seems strange that two weeks before there had not even been any rumours regarding takeovers, but now we felt genuinely disappointed that we were still under the same ownership. Maybe it was now time to be more realistic and hope there would be further investment opportunities in future

In other Championship news, Iain Dowie lost his job as QPR manager after only fifteen games in charge. As it was during his time at Charlton, he had been sacked despite not really having a fair chance. At QPR he had a solid enough start. Despite being one of the richest clubs in the world, they had not spent big money and were only just outside the playoffs. For him to lose his job seemed ridiculous; but it would not have been pleasant

When The Robin Stopped Bobbing

to see him take QPR up, so as a Charlton fan, I felt little sympathy. Next time Dowie gets a job he must be cursing the aftermath of his fifteenth game in charge after lasting the exact same time at both clubs.

The Burnley game I believe was a turning point for Pardew as manager. If we'd got the win, the pressure would have eased greatly, and our league position would have been much more favourable. Even though we came from behind to draw, the performance again was not too great. It was becoming commonplace to boo the team off at half-time. Under Curbishley it was rare for the team to be booed off at half-time or even full-time, but since the midpoint of 2007–8 it was happening far too often.

Todorov scored his first goal since his injury, but this did not cover up the fact we were beginning to look like a very ordinary mid to lower-mid table side. A big positive was the debut of another one of our youngsters, Josh Wright who fitted in well in midfield and looked as though he could cement a place. He had earned good reviews when on loan and had the potential to play regularly in the second tier. Matt Holland had played well for Charlton for a number of years but was showing his age, so it was good to see someone more youthful come in and add competition.

Luke Varney could have won the game and obviously changed everything but after rounding the goalkeeper hit the man on the goal line when it looked easier to score. Varney despite the lack of goals had been our best player since August. One could not fault his work rate, but as a striker he needed a goal.

A draw had stopped serious criticism from the fans, but we needed a run of decent results to ease the pressure on Pardew. Away at Ipswich the following Tuesday we were below par again but somehow nicked a point thanks to Nicky Bailey scoring late. The other Nicky – Weaver – had a mixed night but saved a penalty, so it was difficult to criticise him. He had been almost faultless so far this season.

Even though we didn't deserve a point away at Ipswich, we had not lost, and with relegation-threatened Barnsley up next, a win could have propelled us into mid table. Luckily I had the opportunity to sit in the director's box again. With plenty of speculation surrounding the club about new players and new investment, I was hoping to get some inside info.

Before the game when the team were announced, a lot of the talk was of Darren Ambrose's inclusion in the team. As I said, he was not the fans' favourite, and the speculation was that he was on the verge of leaving on loan with the view to a permanent move away. Unfortunately there was no talk of investment. Josh Wright would also start after being left out against Ipswich, which was good to see, as he was possibly the best player against Burnley.

After forty-five minutes we were 3–0 down. Understandably the Valley erupted into boos and jeers. Sitting near the chairman, I heard many of the fans' criticisms about Pardew. Fans were shouting towards Richard Murray for Pardew to be sacked. Allardyce and Kinsella were mentioned as potential replacements, Even though it was becoming apparent there was need for change, some of the jibes about Pardew were unfair. One or two were claiming Pardew did not care about the club and was a Palace man; this was a cheap shot as you could not question Pardew's desire for things to work out at

Charlton. He may have Palace connections, but played for Charlton, and his commitment was always apparent.

What made things worse was that Barnsley were not that great. They scored their goals from set pieces and showed nothing to suggest they would finish anywhere above lower mid table. We were losing so badly was all our own doing. If it makes sense, we deserved to lose 3–0, but they did not deserve to win 3–0. Barnsley had one or two talented individuals, but we had the better players; and if Charlton played well, we should win.

The final score was 3–1, which left us in the bottom three. At the start of November, the worst I expected was for us to be mid table, but now there were questions of how bad the season could be. Against Barnsley certain individuals let the team down; Ambrose in particular had the look of a player who probably would not play for us again whilst Cranie struggled against Barnsley's aerial threat. Cranie had played well at centre half so far but was not the tallest, and this worked against him. He was not the only player to turn in an awful performance.

If I had to predict the next manager to lose his job, Pardew would have been the favourite, and I could not see him managing at our next home game. The big question though revolves around our finances and whether we could afford to sack him, as this would mean a payoff, and whether we could afford a good enough replacement. I had my doubts over the style of football Allardyce would bring. And since he would command Premiership management wages, he would be out of the question.

Alan Pardew survived though. In our next two games we were the victims of really bad luck. Away at Plymouth we played very well, but after scoring a goal in the ninety-second minute to put us 2–1 up, we blew it and came away with a 2–2. Watching *Soccer Saturday* I thought the result seemed unreal, but a point was at least an improvement on Barnsley. These sorts of occurrences go against only you when you're near the bottom. Pardew must have felt sick coming back from Plymouth as a win would have helped stop the developing Pardew-out bandwagon.

The following Saturday away at Birmingham we turned in a fine performance and were deservedly 2–1 up at half-time. Andy Gray and Bouazza had both scored fine goals, and against a side in second place we had really raised our game. Nevertheless, in the second half two errors cost us, and we lost 3–2. Weaver slipped to gift Phillips an equaliser to start questions over his place in the side, but it seemed as though in a game where we were expected to lose anyway, the performance had bought Pardew more time.

These two away games proved to be turning points in Pardew's tenure. If we had got four to six points, we'd have been in a very healthy position. Although you make your own luck, we had been the victims of some bad luck since the start. Injuries and unlucky goals against had really built up in recent games.

Playing away appeared to be working better, similarly to the start of the previous season when there was not so much pressure on the team. At home it would take only a few misplaced passes or a goal against us for the fans to get nervous and edgy; away there seemed to be more freedom.

Darren Ambrose had unsurprisingly left for Ipswich albeit only on loan whilst we signed Martyn Waghorn on loan from Sunderland. He was very highly rated and had scored goals at all levels except first team but in terms of new players up front, should not have been the priority. At centre half we had struggled since Fortune's injury. Cranie lacked height whilst Primus had not been convincing enough. In midfield Zheng had been missed greatly as there was a lack of quality in there. Bailey had done well, but Sam and Bouazza had been too inconsistent; it was not scoring goals that was a major problem but creating chances.

Up front Gray had done well in terms of goals. Varney had been very unlucky in some games not to have scored more. Dickson had not even started a league game yet, so he'd had no chance to prove his worth. Also with Todorov and McLeod working their way back from long-term injuries, there was enough in attack to suggest if chances were created, we would score enough.

Three days before the Sheffield United game, England played away in Germany. Two ex-Charlton players were on the pitch. Scott Carson played for the national side for the first time since his Croatia howler whilst Darren Bent also was given a run out. Carson unfortunately made another error which gave the Germans the equaliser. As a Charlton fan, you had to feel sorry for him as yet again he had not done himself justice. John Terry came out after the game saying that the goal was his fault, but Carson was by no means blameless to further damage his claims for England Number One.

Darren Bent missed one good chance but did not show enough to suggest he could compete for a regular spot. Nevertheless, at the time of the Germany game, he was in a rich vein of form for Spurs under their new boss, Redknapp. Spurs had an awful start to the season, but Bent still managed a few goals. I thought it was strange when Spurs spent big on more strikers in the window when Bent had shown if he plays, he will score regularly.

Against Sheffield United we could certainly have done with players of Carson's and Bent's ability on the pitch as the Barnsley performance was repeated. By half-time the game was beyond us. In the end we got thrashed 5–2. The game was embarrassing as we were completely outplayed. United had lots of quality shown by their fifth goal – a fine volley from Quinn – but it did not hide the awful defending. After fifty-odd minutes when we were 5–1 down, it was obvious Pardew would go. It was inevitable but still quite sad. Sitting there in a half empty stadium (I never leave early as a rule), all I could think was what if.

What if Pardew had arrived earlier? Would we even be in the Championship? A more recent what-if surrounded the luck we'd had in previous games, especially with Varney's miss against Burnley and the late goal against Plymouth. Also if the best players from the previous season had not been allowed to go, then potentially we could be in the playoffs.

Nevertheless, the game showed Pardew had done all he could, but it was not good enough; Pardew always came across well in interviews and press conferences, so it wasn't nice to see him fail. Walking away from the ground, I thought about potential successors as there was no way he would stay.

During the game one of my flat mates at university thought it would be funny to send a text laughing at our game; understandably this was not taken lightly. We were losing by four goals at home with more than half an hour to go, so to receive a message from someone who claimed to support Man United but had never seen them play or even been to Manchester went beyond a joke. This is not because I am a sore loser (even though I am), but if someone laughs at Charlton and actually knows about football and truly follows a team, that is part of the game. This did not annoy me as much as the actual game, but when you are freezing cold watching your beloved team get thrashed, it is hard to see the funny side. I am not saying you must go to games or even be obsessive about your team to be a real football fan, but it is hard to take someone seriously when they have no connection with the team they support and have no idea about the next fixture.

That Saturday night news broke Pardew had left by mutual consent. His assistant, Phil Parkinson, would act as caretaker while the club searched for an able replacement. Many fans were delighted to see Pardew go; after being a favourite when he arrived, the relationship with the fans had soured.

Pardew ultimately failed at Charlton. Relegation from the top flight was excusable due to the position we were in when he arrived. However, in his one full season, the signings did not perform, and the season as a whole was a major disappointment. The buck has to stop with the manager, and as much as I believed he could have turned it around in 2008–9, the start was not acceptable.

If Andy Reid had been kept, maybe we'd have gone up and he would still have a job. Maybe Pardew could have tried harder to keep him and stand his ground with the board. I think if he had made a stand and risked good relations with the board, the fans would have backed Pardew all the way. We knew how important Reid was to the side. The same could be said to a lesser extent with the departures in summer 2008.

Although he did not spend as much as Dowie did, and of course his signings were not quite so diabolical, Pardew spent a lot of money, and it is hard to think of too many successes. The players who were a success actually were the cheaper signings, such as Semedo, McCarthy and Iwelumo. Some of the money was spend well, including money spent for Bougherra and Zheng, but to spend more than £5 million on three strikers who scored only eleven league goals between them in 2007–8 is exceptionally poor (Varney, McLeod and Gray).

A lot of people believed we would not progress with Pardew in charge. The way the fans felt must have been how West Ham fans did when Pardew left there. What was clear was we were less than halfway through the season and only a few points from mid table. Despite being twenty-second, the situation was retrievable. I'm sure most people who'd seen us play would agree that there's no way we should be in a relegation battle. Neil Warnock had transformed Palace the year before from lower mid table to the playoffs, so there was still the remote possibility that with a new regime and some personnel changes, the season wouldn't be a complete write off.

Billy Davies was the name I wanted as he had done excellent jobs at Preston and Derby, taking the unfancied Preston to the brink of the top flight (only to lose to a certain Alan Pardew side) and then miraculously turned Derby from a lower mid table Championship side to the Premiership. The cynics will say he took charge of Derby's opening games in a season in which they became the worst in Premier League history. However, he admitted the team was not ready. No manager could have saved them from inevitable struggle. He had been rumoured to have been interviewed in 2006, but maybe now the board would realise their mistake.

Ian Holloway was another name mentioned. He had struggled to keep Leicester up the year before and consequently lost his job but had done very well at all his other clubs, including QPR, who he took up from League One and stabilised. Holloway also had worked well with low budgets, including when QPR were in administration, which made him appealing as our finances were tight.

Phil Parkinson had a mixed managerial career. He did exceptionally well in getting Colchester promoted from League One with very limited resources. But at Hull he had struggled to match the fans' and board's ambitions and left them near the bottom of the Championship. As someone who does not believe interior appointments work, I have to admit that ironically one that has is at Hull, where since Parky left in late 2006. His old assistant and replacement, Phil Brown, had done an exceptional job in taking them from the brink of League One to the Premiership.

Phil Parkinson brought in his own players but – perhaps more important – promoted Mark Kinsella and Phil Chapple to have more of an input with the first team. This was good news as both were ex-players and had Charlton in their hearts and understood the club. What was unclear was whether Parkinson would be considered for the job and how long he would have in caretaker charge. What was a worry was that when Reed was given the job, we effectively wrote off the games he was in charge for (except Blackburn). We hoped the next few games would not be similar and any new manager would not come in too late to give us a chance.

Parkinson's first game was away at QPR, who themselves had just appointed a new manager in Paulo Sousa. Sousa had lost his opening game at Watford so was hoping for a response; typically he got one, and QPR won 2–1. But we played a lot better and could have got at least a draw. Luke Varney missed another good chance. But there were plenty of positives. Racon scored on his return from injury whilst Keith Gillespie made his debut after signing on loan the day before.

I do not mind QPR; many fans see them as the Chelsea of the Championship with billionaire owners. They have not spent millions on players and have tried to get promotion the right way. QPR do, however, have issues with owners and after ultimately failing to get promotion in 2009, maybe now they will make the most of their billions. If they go up, QPR will certainly have to improve their stadium.

This game was my first away trip since relegation and first visit to Loftus Road. It is an average Championship stadium but outdated in parts and could certainly do with some Valley-like rejuvenation.

Keith Gillespie was joined by Jay McEveley and Deon Burton in arriving on loan as Parky attempted to make his mark. Not one of these loans really excited the fans. Gillespie and McEveley were solid enough, but Gillespie was no better than what we had, especially given his age and lack of match time this season. At left back Kelly Youga and Grant Basey had struggled to nail a first-team place, so there was need for some freshening up. Youga in particular had a nightmare against Sheffield United, so McEveley, who did not look out of place when he played for Blackburn in the top flight, would add welcome competition.

Deon Burton was particularly uninspiring. Burton would sign for us permanently when the window opened, but it was a clear sign of how our ambitions and finances had dramatically changed as he had never been a regular goal scorer at any of his numerous clubs. And with the quality we had up front, he would not improve the team. His Championship goal ratio especially was less than impressive, and he had scored only one goal this season. Varney may have scored only twice but brought a lot more to the side than goals.

A year before, Burton would not have been seen as good enough for Charlton. Now he was joining on a free and would be potentially our first-choice striker. Sheffield Wednesday, who were mid table with outside playoff ambitions, let him go for free, which shows this was hardly a positive move for the club.

Of course promotion was not going to happen, which meant the parachute payments would end leaving us struggling financially. But there were plenty of players who could be brought in on loan or for nominal fees who would still make a real difference to the team. Watford, who were in a similar position both financially and in terms of the table, brought in one or two players who made a real difference, including Jack Cork and Don Cowie.

To make matters worse, we sold Luke Varney on the same day Burton arrived. He went to Derby on loan, where he would sign permanently. Even though it was not spoken of, it seemed as though Varney was sold only so the club could pay off Pardew. Parkinson said it was because Varney needed a fresh challenge, but he was a potential Premiership player at one point and because of our bad form, his confidence had been shot to pieces. If luck had gone his way, he could have been our top scorer by November. But now we'd sold him for significantly less than the £2.5 million paid in 2007.

This meant since 2006 there were now quite a few players on whom we had made a significant loss, following the likes of Traore and Diawara. Even some of the more recent signings, such as Gray and McLeod, would not demand anywhere near the same money as Charlton paid.

Another reason why these signings did not inspire – aside from the fact they didn't look good enough (except maybe McEveley) – was that it seemed as though they were only brought in so Parkinson could stamp his mark on the club. We needed reinforcements but not just anyone that was available. The squad we had was not that bad where any new player could walk into the side and do a better job. Any new manager would have looked at the current squad and assessed who would improve and strengthen.

Two days after these transfers, at home to Southampton we came up against a fine goalkeeping performance from Kelvin Davies. Gillespie was lively out wide, and McEveley did well at left back, but Southampton were in deep trouble. Not to beat them was disappointing. We deserved the points but couldn't break through. Jon Fortune returned, and we kept our first clean sheet since he last played in September. Racon suffered another injury. Every time we got some good news there would be something to ruin it.

The following week we went bottom of the league for the first time after losing at Blackpool. The result was deserving of a poor performance to suggest whoever the manager was, similar to late 2006, the squad needed improving. Unlike 2006 Arsenal probably would not help us out by loaning any fringe players. Alex Song, who'd been superb for us, was really starting to establish himself in Arsenal's midfield alongside Fabregas. It would be nice to have a player or two with similar potential.

After losing at Blackpool it took a few minutes for it to sink in that we were bottom of the league. The Premiership was like a different life now as it was looking like staying up would be a relief rather than a given. To make matters worse, the player who won the game for Blackpool – Liam Dickinson – was only at the club on loan from Derby following their signing of Varney.

Going into the game against Coventry at the Valley as the bottom team was still a shock as we attempted to get off the bottom. There was no throwing in the towel though as a win could have drawn us level on points with Watford in twenty-first. Coventry were not in great form, and after a positive home performance against Southampton, we were in reasonable spirits. I would not say the match had a must-win feel to it, but of course a home game against a side like Coventry does usually require a healthy result no matter where you are in the league.

The Coventry game produced one of the worst performances of the season; the team did not respond and were rightly booed off. After we had drawn level for about a minute, Coventry scored a fine free kick, and we couldn't recover. Deon Burton scored, but it was a penalty earned by Izale McLeod in only his fourth league start since signing. McLeod actually did OK, considering his lack of match time, but was forced to play out wide in the second half.

The goal to win the game could have been attributed to poor goalkeeping from Nicky Weaver as the free kick was a long way out and Weaver's positioning was not the best. Despite lacking confidence Weaver had been better after blips against Birmingham and Sheffield United. At home to Southampton, he stopped them getting an undeserved victory with a good double save after being left vulnerable by a leaky defence.

At the end the fans turned on the players with chants of 'You're not fit to wear the shirt'. This was more than fair as even though the management had been questionable, there was no doubt in my mind that the teams selected had been good enough to win more than they had. Going back to uni, I felt angry that things had got so bad. We had a few massive games coming up to stop us getting cut adrift, starting at home to Derby.

Before the Derby game it was announced Phil Parkinson would be the manager throughout the festive period. I still believed we needed a new manager altogether, but the decision seemed a sensible one. The players would at least have some stability for some vital games, and this would give the board time to ensure there are no rash decisions.

When explaining this decision, Richard Murray talked of the precarious financial situation following relegation. Slightly confusing was why, after overspending in 2006 and then paying the price, did the board then sanction another overspend to try to ensure a swift return. Surely they should have learned their lessons. At the time it was evident that spending so much may have been a slight risk (especially around £5 million on Varney, McLeod and Zheng). But following a hefty fee for Darren Bent this did not seem as though it could jeopardise our future and raise concerns over the dreaded administration.

On the plus side. in the match-day programme, there was talk from Derek Chappell, the PLC chairman, about some recent enquiries for investment. This was positive to hear as even though there would be no billionaire Zabeel, any investment would be more than welcome.

Derby had been struggling themselves since relegation from the Premiership. They could not seem to find enough consistency to match their fans' ambitions (sounds familiar). The match would be live on *Sky*, so Conor and I decided to dress up as Santa. The only real motivation for this was to get on television and bring some light to a dark situation. It was also our last home game before Christmas. Never before have I made such an effort to get ready for Charlton, and it was well worth it. We were a little overshadowed by another group of fans who held up a banner with 'All I want for Xmas is three points'. But we were still caught by the cameras on more than one occasion.

In the actual game we played very well and fully deserved to win but were denied by a late, late leveller. Before the match started it was announced Rob Elliot would debut in goal, the reasons for this was a combination of Weaver needing a rest and carrying an injury. Martyn Waghorn would also start his first home game before he was due to return to Sunderland.

Parkinson understandably knew he needed a reaction, so there was no surprise he had shaken things up.

With ninety minutes on the clock we were winning 2–1. To be fair, Derby were awful, but there still were numerous positives. Rob Elliot looked assured in goal. He made one good save and looked confident and commanding unlike Weaver who clearly had been lacking confidence when coming for crosses. He certainly was not to blame for the goals. Up front Gray and Waghorn linked up well together and both got a goal. Gray's opener was the type that he scored on several occasions for his previous club as he excellently turned his man in the box before firing home (the kind of goal you expect from a complete Championship striker). After Derby equalised through a penalty, we responded terrifically and scored another almost immediately, Waghorn finding space in the box after Lloyd Sam's cutback.

However in the last minute of four added on, Ellington reacted quickest to a flick in the box to make it 2–2. This was up there with Fulham for feeling sick. We fully deserved three points, but one lapse in concentration cost us dear and meant we had not won for fourteen games. There was some annoyance at the defending for the last minute goal whilst Bouazza especially had missed a guilt edged chance to put us two goals up.

The feeling of disappointment was awful, a win really would have galvanised the players and given the whole club such a lift. But having applauded the team off and sat miserably for a couple of minutes in my seat, I spotted a camera so started pointing upwards and kissing my badge, pretty certain I was saying, 'We still believe; we're staying up; no problem'.

When I got home and watched the match back, Sky showed me in my costume pointing at the sky kissing my Charlton badge. This was only mere consolation for the injustice of the game as Derby had stolen a point. But it was quite good to be on TV.

Martyn Waghorn had impressed against Derby not just with his goal but he had good movement and looked lively. After the Derby game his loan was extended for another month, which was good news. Although he would no doubt return to Sunderland as at only eighteen he has a long career ahead, it was good to keep him as in one game he looked more of a goal threat than our other frontmen had in recent weeks.

After almost everyone in the squad having had a chance to stake a claim for a spot, but after the Derby game Chris Dickson, who'd never started a game and had made only eight sub appearances, requested a transfer. It seemed strange he had not been given a chance, especially after scoring lots for Gills in the league below and would possibly be the type of player who'd come back to haunt us.

One player who definitely fell into this category was Leroy Lita. After being a reasonably decent loan signing for us, he had gone to Norwich and done very well. Unsurprisingly he scored the winner against us in our next game at Carrow Road.

After deserving a win against Derby, we had high hopes going into the game against another fellow struggler. The performance was not bad, but slow defending cost us, and we didn't threaten their leaky defence enough. The draw against Derby had taken us off the bottom. But with two tricky-looking games just after Christmas, we were a long way from safety.

Chapter 11

THE FULL-TIME CARETAKER

QPR on Boxing Day was never going to be easy. They were on the brink of the playoffs. From the outside it appeared as though the decision to replace Iain Dowie with Paulo Sousa was being justified. However, they were not unbeatable, and if we could reproduce the form of the Derby game, we'd have a chance.

Going to the Valley on Boxing Day is always well worth it. Normally the fixtures mean we have a London Derby, so there is always a cracking atmosphere from both sides. Charlton and QPR do not have a great rivalry, but they still brought a couple of thousand fans to the Valley, and the match was certainly one of the more exciting of the season.

We did not win to extend our winless run, but after coming back from 1–0 and 2–1, down to level it was certainly a point earned rather than two lost. Lee Cook carried on from Lita for ex-loanees to score against us with a terrific free kick. Blackstock took advantage of some poor defending to give us an uphill task. Even so, a great deal or credit must go to the players for twice fighting back, Bailey scored two headers, and we should have won the game but Sam missed a simple header.

Phil Parkinson showed his passion for the cause by getting sent to the stands for protesting against the referee for denying us at least two clear penalties. We were robbed of these decisions, and Parky was spot on in his criticism of the referee. On the negative side, we were now only one loss or draw from equalling a club record for winless games (sixteen) and were back to the bottom of the league after other results.

Keith Gillespie returned to Sheffield United after his loan. He would not be missed as he'd done nothing to suggest he'd be an asset if kept. Gillespie is obviously a good player; he showed that with his volley against us in 2006. But at the Valley apart from a decent first half against Southampton, he did not do enough. Sam looked the more threatening of the two wingers.

Sam was excellent against Derby and QPR. Parkinson said that if he could improve consistency, there is no reason why he cannot play in the top flight. With tremendous pace and the ability to beat a man, if his final ball improves, he is not far off being as good as someone like Steven Pienaar. At times in 2007–8, Sam was a constant menace to the opposition and weighed in with one or two important goals. These goals were not frequent enough though.

Against Sheffield United we played well in the first half but sat back in the second and caved in, losing 3–1. There was no surprise in defeat as Sheffield United were flying high. We played with a negative formation with only Burton up front and invited the pressure. We had equalled the club record of winless games, and the players had not reacted to Alan Pardew's departure in the desired way.

After eight games in caretaker charge and no wins, Parkinson, the board decided, was the right man to lead us to survival and was named permanent manager. This was not the most popular decision amongst supporters, especially as Parkinson's record as caretaker was identical to Pardew's last 8 games (5 defeats and 3 draws). There was also the wide school of though that Parkinson was the cheap option as he was already contracted to the club and any new appointment would have meant spending valuable funds.I believed the squad was good enough to stay up but this did not change the fact that it needed freshening up, especially at the back. Therefore the funds saved from appointing a new manager would be more than welcomed and hopefully mean we could afford a couple of permanent signings rather than even more loans.

In support of Parkinson, his time in caretaker had included plenty of bad luck. Certainly we deserved to beat Southampton, Derby and QPR at home and we would have done but for some good goalkeeping and poor finishing. If we had won even just two of his games in charge then Parkinson would be hailed as a potential messiah and going into 2009, the fans would have been looking upwards.

Even though I am not and never will be a fan of interior appointments when a manager leaves, the fact Parkinson knew the squad inside out was a major advantage. If a new manager had come in, it would have taken him time to get to know the players and make his mark. With a busy January, this was time Charlton did not have as we needed points and players.

Parkinson had also inherited a club in massive turmoil and unlike Les Reed, he had good managerial experience. In 2006, Parky was even considered for the Charlton job after working miracles with Colchester and forming a fine reputation as one of the brightest young managers around.

Parkinson's first match as permanent manager would be at home to Norwich in the cup. Like us they would be more focussed on the league, so it was a good opportunity to get a first win since 4 October. Some of the youngsters would get a chance to stake a claim. Maybe the game would be a much needed confidence booster.

Before the game Martin Cranie returned to Pompey after his loan expired. He would not be missed by some fans, but I thought he had done well at right back and in some games at centre back. If he were a bit taller, he'd be a top defender. Linvoy Primus had gone back about a month before after not being able to force his way into the side. So there was now room for new faces.

One unexpected return to the Valley was Darren Ambrose, who'd failed to shine at Ipswich, so they sent him back. Few fans were pleased to see him back, but as someone with ability, there was always the hope that the loan spell may have improved him and we could have a whole new player. One player I'd like to have seen return was Luke Varney. But his loan became permanent now the window was open as did Burton's.

Against Norwich the performance was quite good. Jonjo Shelvey enhanced his personal reputation with a cracking goal; but we could not hold on, and a replay was required. This meant the current side had broken the record for the longest winless game streak; this side were now officially the worst in Charlton's history.

When Parkinson got the job full time, there was much emphasis on the next league game at home to Nottingham Forest. They were five points ahead of us, so a home win would really open things up near the bottom and maybe lift us off the bottom. Forest had sacked their manager, Colin Calderwood, after a poor run of results and appointed Billy Davies. It would be his first proper match in charge after being in the stand for their FA Cup win at billionaires' Man City. This meant they would go into the game in high spirits.

In the lead up to the game, it was two in one out at the Valley. Graham Murty signed from Reading on loan. He would bring plenty of experience to the club and possibly shore up the defence even more. To be fair to Pardew, we had not been shipping as many goals since he came in. Leaving was Hameur Bouazza after he decided he would rather go on loan to Birmingham, who were near the top. He had shown a clear lack of loyalty to the club. But as with many of the loans, no tears were shed.

Bouazza had talent but was inconsistent and did not have the necessary desire or character. One thing that sticks in my mind is against Sheffield United in Pardew's last game, he went in half-heartedly to a challenge which led their opener. To watch him was immensely frustrating as shown when he missed a sitter to seal the Derby game. I hoped that he would prove to Birmingham what he had to us that he was unprofessional and not up for the fight. Bouazza would join Marcus Bent, Scott Sinclair and Djimi Traore in a Birmingham squad littered with players who'd not shone at the Valley.

When The Robin Stopped Bobbing

The day before the Forest game we signed Matt Spring on a permanent deal. This was another very uninspiring signing as Spring was solid enough in centre midfield but was nothing better than what we already had. Zheng and Racon were near fitness, so the centre midfield was perhaps our strongest area, especially given Bailey's good form and Semedo, Holland and Wright to increase the competition.

Against Forest we started well, but Burton showed why he has never scored goals prolifically, with two misses, when he should have done better, first hitting the side netting and then the goalkeeper. We paid for this as Forest scored two before half-time; both were embarrassing goals to concede after individual errors. The second was a terrible mistake from Holland as his back header was never going through to the keeper and gifted Earnshaw a goal. At times the performance bordered on humiliating as after they scored a second, Forest really did not have to do much to ensure the win. It felt as though in the second half there were not enough adjectives to describe how bad it was.

Matt Holland had been tremendous in his years with the club, but this year he had struggled to make his mark on games. He had lost a yard of pace and mobility. Parkinson needed to be ruthless as Holland's performance against Forest was substandard. Despite being a cult hero at the club, he was no longer good enough for a Championship midfield. I do not enjoy writing this about Holland as his loyalty has been fantastic and he was one of our best players in the latter Premiership years. To be fair to Holland, he always gave 100 per cent, and his commitment was never questioned, unlike certain other players.

Darren Ambrose somehow got his place back in the team and showed nothing to suggest he had improved as he made not mark, did not get on the ball enough and went missing too often. The left-hand side of midfield was now a massive problem for us as we had no natural replacement for Bouazza and Parkinson seemed reluctant to play Grant Basey on the left even though he did well there against Coventry on the last day of 2007–8.

During a game the club normally has an advert on the big screen with a fish going across the screen. I have no idea what the advert is for, but it is more notable for the fact the home fans usually shout 'Fiiissshh' This is because we had Mark Fish playing for us for a number of years. Fish was not the best defender but was still decent and, like many of Curbs' signings, was a bargain and reliable. With League One looming, the club continued with this advert, which was crazy. Not only is it a cheap way to try to inspire fans but it is also very irritating and a reminder of former glories when Fish was a mainstay in a successful Charlton side.

The only positive was another good performance from Shelvey; he looked a class above the rest of the team. When your best player by a long stretch is sixteen, it shows how bad things are. Whatever league we'd be in the next year, it was evident that he'd be linked with top-flight clubs, and it would be hard to keep hold of him. The defeat left us eight points behind Forest, and the safety margin was a long way off. To make matters worse, we Semedo was out for at least the next two months to join the list of absentees.

Billy Davies had shown how the appointment of a new manager can have an instant impact. Davies said he was close to being our manager in 2006 but decided against it, further suggesting Dowie was not even the second choice as rumours were that Peter Taylor was also ahead of Dowie. After starting well with Forest, Davies was a manager that we'd regret not taking.

Forest was a real low in the season. To have virtually lost our most important game of the season by half-time was a massive blow. Parkinson was in no way flavour of the month, but after the way some of the players were performing it begged the question whether any manager could have the desired impact.

A win away at Norwich in the cup replay merely acted as cover for our league form. A first win in nineteen was nothing to be proud of, especially as Norwich were awful. The next day they sacked their manager, Glenn Roeder, to add to Watford and Nottingham Forest for replacing their managers with completely new regimes to try to ensure survival. Similar to the Derby game, our own good performance did not hide the fact the other teams contributed just as much to the results.

It was, however, just nice to win a game. Many of the youngsters had played and done well; this boded well for the next few games. Ambrose scored his first of the season to frustrate fans even more as his ability had been shown in a cup game rather than a vital league match.

Before the Wednesday game we signed Tom Soares on loan from Stoke. This was a real coup as he had done well for Palace in the Championship and possibly had other loan options from teams in much better situations. Less than three months previously Soares had played for

Stoke against Spurs in the Premiership and looked every inch a top-flight player, so the hope was unlike most of the other loans he could make a real impact – unlike most of the other loans.

Izale McLeod left for Millwall on loan till the end of the year whilst McEveley and Waghorn returned to their clubs. McLeod had never been given a fair crack at Charlton. He had played only the full ninety minutes on one occasion in the league. After struggling with the demands of the Championship, League One maybe would be a good level for him to get some goals and come back full of confidence whatever league we'd be in. If Tom Soares played, he would be the thirty-fifth player to represent the club already this season. This showed how we had not improved on the last season in terms of stability and continuity. Thirty-five players by mid January is not a good statistic.

All the positivity that came from the Norwich game was destroyed after one half at Sheffield Wednesday. We would eventually lose 4–1 in a game where Parkinson's team selection baffled the fans as much as the result did. After winning at Norwich with some of the younger players, Parky decided to bring back Spring after his unproductive debut against Forest whilst Tom Soares walked straight into the side. Ambrose, who'd scored on the Tuesday, was left out as was Josh Wright who'd had another impressive game in midfield.

Robert Elliot had done well since coming into the side; he had made some good saves and certainly did not disgrace himself. However, after Elliot was rested for the Norwich game, Darren Randolph kept his place at Hillsborough. In another dire game, Randolph made some good saves but still conceded four goals. Parkinson's erratic team selections left the question who would play in goal for the remainder of the season.

Our next game was the fourth round of the cup against Sheffield United. As much as the league remained the priority, a win would still have been nice. It could give us confidence, a Premiership tie in the next round and some much needed money. It appeared that it may be a while before we'd be competing with the top sides again, but an away tie would be nice against one of the top four.

Sheffield United predictably won the game. But after the two league games when we'd lost comprehensively, this was a lot closer. With a bit more luck, we could have earned a replay. However, a loss was not really a bad thing, and we played better than the Wednesday game. Chris Dickson came on as substitute and scored a decent goal to reinforce his claims for a fair chance. The transfer window was nearly closed, and there had not been any significant interest in him, so maybe after a goal he would still have a role to play.

After the game there were reports of a fallout between Phil Parkinson and Josh Wright after the player was told he would not start the game. Despite only being a newspaper report regarding the player refusing to play, Wright did not get another look in and was loaned to Gillingham for the remainder of the season. He did very well at Gills as he helped them to playoff success to further question why we spent valuable funds on Matt Spring when we had an abundance of centre midfielders who actually had not done a lot wrong. Nicky Bailey had been one of the stand-out performers. With Racon and Semedo also in contention, when looking at areas to fund, the left of midfield and at centre half, where there was only two recognised centre halfs, should have been the focus for any player investment.

Phil Parkinson is the manager; so his decisions have to be accepted even if they aren't respected. If Wright crossed a line, then fair play to Parkinson for stamping authority and taking charge of the situation. I am sure many players air their frustrations about not playing, but as a young player, Wright should maybe have gone about things differently.

The cup win against Norwich was a welcome relief but did not change the fact we had not won in the league since early October. Our next match was the perfect match to end our awful run at home to Crystal Palace. Surely here the players would need no motivation. A win could prove to be the catalyst for a great escape; a big ask, but Palace had not replicated their success from the last season, so three points was not mission impossible. On the other hand, a defeat could really stick the knife in. The Palace game was on a Tuesday night, so there would be a marvellous atmosphere. They'd bring a fair few whilst our fans would be in good voice regardless of the league standings.

The morning of the game I felt as though I would be playing in the game. I was so nervous. I hate to admit it, but travelling up to London I expected us to lose. The Ipswich win was such a long time ago. Ever since I had considered changing all my prematch rituals, but nothing had been able to change our fortunes on the pitch. Wearing lucky shirts and socks as well as always

When The Robin Stopped Bobbing

having a hot dog from the same stall had for a long time proved not to be working.

After Charlton fans continually singing 'We sent the Palace down' after the events of 2005, the away fans decided to have their own version to the chorus of Amarillo. For most of the game, they would be singing 'Who the fuck is laughing now'. To be fair, they were right. We had laughed at their plight when we were sitting pretty, but now just under four years after the event, the roles had been well and truly reversed. It was clear this was our biggest match since relegation from the Premiership; three points were a must.

After Matt Spring scored a fantastic volley early on, we spent the next seventy-five minutes hanging on. To say it was nerve-wracking would be a massive understatement as we struggled to get out of our half. Palace did not actually create that much, and Rob Elliot had to make only a couple of saves. Mark Hudson against his former club was colossal as was Jon Fortune until he got taken off injured. Andy Gray played well up front as he held the ball up terrifically and dropped back into midfield when he needed to. Unfortunately, like Fortune, he was taken off injured. Both would be ruled out for the season to take some of the gloss off a famous win.

Matt Spring may not have been the most popular of signings, but his goal was very well taken. As the ball dropped on his left foot he could have easily snatched at the chance, but credit to him, he finished brilliantly. Also in midfield Tom Soares, playing against his former club, showed no sentiment as he turned in a great performance in an unfamiliar right-hand side role.

Towards the end I don't think I have ever been so nervous, especially when there were five added minutes. The Derby game was still too fresh in the memory. The referee was possibly influenced by Warnock as he seemed determined to give Palace as many chances as possible to attack. In late injury time, the ball was being fairly held up in the corner, and unexplainably the ref gave them one of many dubious free kicks.

A first league win in eighteen could not have come against a better side. We still remained eight points off safety, but even if we did get relegated, the season would have a clear highlight. There was the feeling that it was too little too late, but for one night it felt as though we'd won a cup final. Going back to uni, I think I was the happiest I'd been in a long while. With the tune of 'Valley Floyd Road' still fresh in my head, it was almost forgotten that this was the worst Charlton side for many years and League One was beckoning.

Neil Warnock predictably did not take the defeat with dignity and decided to have a go at our players and the officials. Admittedly we sat back and wasted a bit of time, but Warnock's comments about how much time we wasted were highly exaggerated. According to him there should have been fifteen added on. Warnock also slated our players for their attitude under Pardew and said that if they'd put in the same amount of effort with him, we wouldn't be bottom. He was right, but after a defeat he could have accepted it rather than saying the players should be disgusted with themselves. This was not the time nor was it Warnock's place to evaluate the problems with Charlton. It was hardly as if Palace were going up or were a team we should look to follow.

The injuries were massive blows as we had been more solid with Fortune in the side, and with a lack of cover he would certainly be missed. Pardew had said of Fortune that over the years a lack of consistency had been his problem, but there was a stage when in the Premiership that he looked a top defender. One year he was linked with clubs such as Newcastle, especially after having a fantastic game against Alan Shearer.

Andy Gray may not have been a fans' favourite but was still the top scorer and against Palace gave the kind of performance which he'd given for years in the Championship. He would also be missed. Gray needed the right service to score goals and at times this season had got it, either from wide areas or balls to feet. Gray had scored for Burnley and Sunderland against Charlton after good service, but since his arrival this had not been forthcoming.

Similarly with Chris Iwelumo, who started the season on fire, as he reached double figures by October, suffered from the same problem at the Valley. When he got the service, his record for us was impressive, but as soon as this stopped so did the goals. In his early spell at Wolves, they had two of the league's best wingers in Kightly and Jarvis supplying crosses for him to get his head on.

Following the Palace game, I got in touch with a friend who I'd known at school; we were both Charlton fans and used to discuss the club all the time. I'm pretty sure we lost contact around the time Charlton began to struggle, so maybe it was a good omen that we'd started speaking again. Tom, like me, had been going to Charlton for a number of years, and we seemed to agree on where it had gone wrong and who was to blame.

Certainly it was good to know there was someone else to moan about Charlton with and assess the rights and wrongs of the last couple of seasons. Immediately Tom reminded me of the glory years when we debated whether players such as Kishishev were actually any good for the top flight. Unlike me, he was not such a fan of Kish or J.J., but now I'm sure both of us would welcome them back.

Our next game away at playoff-chasing Burnley would be tough. With Hudson joining the injury list, the two loan signings we brought in were welcomed. Darren Ward especially was needed as there were no fit centre halfs whilst Tresor Kandol would help deal with the loss of Gray. Kandol was not the most convincing of signings. According to Leeds fans, he was average in League One. But we needed someone to hold the ball up and act as a target man.

Burnley had playoff aspirations, but after phenomenal cup runs when they beat a number of top-flight London sides, their league form was a bit patchy, so another healthy result was not beyond impossibilities. Owen Coyle had done a fantastic job there with one of the smallest budgets in the league. Having seen them play a couple of times both against Charlton and on Sky, I thought their promotion to the Premiership was almost a bigger shock than Hull's the year before.

Chris Dickson got his first start for Charlton after he had impressed as a substitute. He played very well and set up our goal. But after conceding two goals very late, the familiar feeling of disappointment had returned. Burnley scored their winner late into six minutes of added time to leave us feeling sick. A draw would have carried on from

Palace and given us decent impetuous, but it seemed as though we'd gone back to square one.

The following Tuesday we played away at Bristol City in another tough game; in almost a repeat of the Burnley game, we came away feeling pig sick. In the first half, we played very well and deservedly went a goal up through Soares. On *Soccer Special* on Sky Sports, every time the reporter described our game it seemed that our front two, especially Dickson with his pace, were causing their defence all sorts of problems. The only downside was that it was only a one-goal lead, and there was no way our defence could be relied on to hold out.

Two goals in a very short space of time cost us dearly, Dele Adebola scoring two goals to highlight the loss of Hudson and our weaknesses. Matt Holland had filled in admirably at centre half but lacked height and could not contain the aerial threat of Adebola. The goals were not as late as at Burnley, but for the second game in a row, we had thrown away the chance of a good result. Safety was miles away. The performance in the second half was not good enough as City could have had even more, and we did not match the same levels reached against Palace.

The following week a home game against Cardiff was postponed due to snowfall and safety reasons for away fans travelling from Wales. Our game was one of many called off after awful weather all around the country. Although it is not right, I was pleased our game was off and welcomed a weekend away from the worry. Cardiff were in good form and had a good chance of promotion whilst had only won only one game since early October. The hope was that by the time the game would be played in late April, we would have picked up a lot and maybe

Cardiff would have faltered. The postponement also gave us a game in hand over our rivals. Of course I would rather have the points, but it does give the table a better look when you know you have a chance to gain ground on others.

One win since October became two at home to Plymouth in a game where we possibly turned out our best performance since the Reading game. Some important players delivered good performances. After sneaking a win against Palace, some of us believed again. Thierry Racon, who'd only just returned from injury, look very accomplished in midfield and scored a wonderful opener with his weaker left foot. Racon needed time to adjust to the English game, but it appeared after a year that when he was playing, the team played better. Bailey played on the left and actually did well; although not a long-term solution out wide, he got just as involved on the left and scored a fine goal, latching on to a flick from Kandol, who also impressed on his home debut.

Arguably the man of the match, however, was Chris Dickson. The game really begged the question about why it had taken so long for him to get a start. He may not have been ready in 2007, but surely judging by his performances in recent weeks, he looked more of a threat than most of our other strikers had in the whole season. Since Varney left this was the first time we saw a striker with genuine pace cause so many problems. Couple this with a terrific work rate, and there was the making of a good Championship striker. For the umpteenth time since we'd been relegated. there looked to be the making of a good partnership up front as Kandol also had a terrific game linking up well and assisting Bailey for the second.

Plymouth were awful and looked in trouble themselves. We were now seven points from safety and with some vital home games on the agenda, had a glimmer of hope. Southampton lost at Bristol City, so we were also now only a win away from being off the bottom of the league for the first time since Boxing Day.

Our next game was away at fellow strugglers Barnsley. In an uneventful match, a 0–0 was a decent result, and at least the abysmal away run was over. We had not picked up a point since early November. Coincidentally, on the same day Manchester United conceded their first league goal since they lost to Arsenal, we last got an away point at Plymouth.

Having seen Manchester play live at Old Trafford a few days before as they comfortably overcame Fulham, I could not help but be impressed. This was the first Premiership match I had been to since May 2007, and I could see the gap between the top flight and Championship. At times United were almost unplayable. Paul Scholes especially had a phenomenal game. He not only scored a fine goal but his passing and awareness were sublime. This was the time when people were talking about this United side being the best ever and predicting them to win at least four major trophies. On this evidence it was hard to argue.

Fulham, on the other hand, had the look of a Charlton side of old. They were outclassed at times but remained disciplined and spirited; they could have scored themselves as well. After Chris Coleman was sacked, they found themselves in almost an identical position to

Charlton the year before when Sanchez left in December 2007. Unlike with Charlton though, Roy Hodgson led them to a great escape and since has reaped the rewards of top-flight football with an attractive brand of football and some cracking players. When looking at Fulham's form over the last couple of seasons, as a Charlton fan I cannot help but think that could have been us. Of course the same could be said looking at West Ham or Wigan, who also only just survived when we were relegated. But Fulham have a similar fan base, and we are probably similar-sized clubs. If things had been a bit different, in late 2008 we'd be in Europe whilst they'd be playing Gillingham.

Following a good result against Barnsley, we then went to Swansea and got an even more pleasing point. Swansea were renowned for their ball playing philosophy and looked a good bet for the playoffs. Their home form was also amongst the league's best, so a draw was a terrific result. Bailey scored again after playing on the left to make him our top scorer. We should have scored again through Ambrose, but a point was more than welcomed.

It did appear though, that things were on the up. The performances had improved no end and to go to Barnsley and Swansea, where we would have certainly lost a few weeks before, was exceptionally satisfying. Parkinson was now having a positive impact and the players seemingly were responding.

Watching *Soccer Saturday*, I saw that the only negative was that all the other results went against Charlton. Southampton surprisingly won against Cardiff, Forest, Watford and Doncaster won. This meant that a point now seemed a bit of a letdown as we'd not moved any further forward.

The other results put tremendous pressure on our next two fixtures. Both were at home to relegation rivals in Doncaster and Watford (proverbial massive six pointers). Personally I believed we needed at least 4 points to give us any hope. Anything less and that would be that for our Championship stay.

Chapter 12

How Did Things Get This Bad?

The game against Doncaster had a real must-win feel about it. They were in good form, after looking doomed around Christmas, but after two home wins on the bounce we had to fancy our chances. As did Swansea, Donny played an exciting attractive style of football, so it would not be easy.

Graham Murty had gone back to Reading after injury. To be fair, he had played well and been one of the more successful loans; we immediately replaced him with the signing of Danny Butterfield on loan from Palace. Yassin Moutaouakil must have been feeling pretty annoyed that he kept being overlooked for the first team as since his arrival we had tried numerous right backs. Mouts had a run in the side towards the end of Pardew's tenure and had looked no worse than any of the other loans. He may not be the best defensively, but if this had been worked on, he could have been one of the best fullbacks in the league. The thought of him and Sam terrorising left backs does seem like an opportunity lost.

Against Doncaster we did not deserve any more than the 2–1 defeat; despite having plenty of shots, more poor defending cost us. Bailey had dragged us back into the game before then ruining this by giving away a stupid penalty. Bailey had been superb since arriving; but he is too rash in some of his challenges, and this was highlighted in the Donny game. They scored from the spot, and we'd lost our most important game of the season.

When Bailey equalised a lot of time remained, and with the impetuous we should have really pressurised them. Instead, after they scored again, Neil Sullivan in Doncaster's goal was not tested again. The pressure on the team had got to the players as they could not carry on our recent upturn at home. The fans were in good voice but it made no difference.

Leaving the ground, I felt the same atmosphere as after the Sheffield United game in April 2007; relegation was a virtual certainty. Playing in League One only two years after playing in the top tier was a horrible feeling. In terms of size we may not be a Premier League club, but there is no way Charlton belong in the third level. Only a few years before we'd been four divisions above Doncaster. Now they'd be above us, which summed up how far we'd fallen away.

At Swansea Kandol did not play due to personal reasons. Shelvey came in to support Dickson. Parky stuck with this at home to Doncaster and was too negative. Dickson struggled and lost more and more confidence as the game went on; in all fairness, he was up front on his own and does not really have the necessary attributes to play the role successfully, especially when there is a lack of support from the wingers. If we had two natural wingers who could get up and down the pitch, the formation may have worked as seen when Thomas and Sam played up with Iwelumo.

Not saying that if we played with a more natural 4–4–2 we'd have beaten Doncaster; but in a match which we really needed the win, a more positive look would have been better received. Parkinson admitted afterwards that we faced an uphill struggle to stay up. As much as this was obvious, to hear our manager virtually throw in the towel was not good to hear.

Against Doncaster, like many clubs, Charlton had given away cheap tickets to try to keep attendances up. This is great when the team is doing well, but when the side is struggling and emotions are running high, in my view it is not the best idea to have supports who do not truly understand what the hardcore fans are going through. For example, in the Donny match during a chorus of 'Valley Floyd Road', a guy who was not a regular commented that some fans in our block were showing off because they were singing loudly and passionately. The song has no bad language and is our most recognisable song. To say people singing it is showing off, highlights how some people at football have no idea of the emotions fans go through. Having been a fan for so long, I of course know the whole song and tend to join in. My block is not the most vocal in the stadium, and we do unfortunately get people who turn up just to watch a game.

On Boxing Day against QPR, some Spurs fans had no clue and gave the regulars weird looks. I know because I have done the same at other grounds. I went to see

Arsenal play Hull in the FA Cup, and most of the match it was very frustrating. Some fans near me were kicking every ball and looked like giving themselves heart attacks. Seeing them act this way, I, a non-Arsenal fan, was reminded of how I feel at Charlton sometimes. As a fan you can choose the level of obsession and how seriously you take it. Since our seasons have involved relegation battles, the games have become more important, and a win or loss would dictate the rest of the week.

Parkinson carried on from Pardew by being too inconsistent in his team selection. After one poor game, Chris Dickson was not even in the sixteen. Over the last two years, there had been too many instances when the manager would drop a player after one bad game. Yassin and Grant Basey were the prime examples of this. Both had ability but were relatively young and inexperienced, so average performances were to be expected. At time it was almost as if the managers were waiting for them to make a mistake and drop them. Every time Mouts would not play well he'd be out of the side and a new loan would come in (Scunthorpe February '08 and Preston August '08).

Grant Basey had done very well when he first broke into the side but since has not been able to cement a place despite not doing much wrong. Kelly Youga, who has often been selected ahead of him, has been more inconsistent and makes too many mistakes; in my view he can be a liability at the back and gets caught out of position too often. Basey although lacking pace is more solid and offers a good threat going forward. At the start of the season, he helped set up a few of our goals with excellent set-piece delivery. Basey also impressed on the left of midfield and in a central role but had not been able to build on this.

Chris Dickson had played only six Championship games in a bottom of the table side, so surely he needed more games to prove himself. He had been unlucky not to score and had still looked more of a goal threat than our others forwards did, especially when you consider Burton was yet to score from open play and Todorov was not fit enough.

It seemed questionable as to why some players were given numerous chances to prove themselves and find the necessary consistency, whereas others were perhaps not fancied by the manager and have not been cut enough slack. If the two managers had been less unpredictable with their teams, the players would not have let them down so often and the performances would have been better.

The Watford game four days later was equally disappointing. Before the game we were twelve points from safety, so it was win or bust. Even a win would probably not have been enough but would have given us a fighting chance. Brendan Rodgers had transformed Watford since taking over, and similar to Doncaster they arrived in good form.

In the match-day programme, Darren Ambrose did an interview which was more than interesting; it was almost three pages of him talking about his injuries followed by him saying how much he loved the club. It appeared as though Ambrose were trying to get the fans off his back. His injuries might have affected his form, but this does not change the fact he had at times been awful when playing for Charlton and has never shown the ability he clearly possesses. The talk of how he loved the club was bullshit as he'd obviously be leaving in the summer regardless of what league we'd be in.

We would certainly be in League One. Watford scored their opener after abysmal defending when they opened us up. But we fought back. Kandol scored two goals to become the first Charlton striker to score for the club since Andy Gray against Derby the previous December.

In the second half we threw it away. More poor defending gifted them the victory. Mark Hudson especially did not cover himself in glory for the winner. As much as he had some good games for the club, Hudson was a major letdown over the course of the season. His Palace form suggested he could play in the Premiership, but too often his lack of pace and mobility had been exposed. As captain he had to take a great deal of responsibility for our poor defensive record. On the other hand, Hudson was not the worst defender to play for us and had some fine games, particularly against Palace. But like many others, he did not play to the level he could have done.

Also in defence was Danny Butterfield, who'd been less than impressive in his opening games. He was another player from Palace, which angered many fans. Since 2006 too many with strong links to Palace had come to Charlton and contributed to our downfall (Alan Pardew is excluded in my opinion). At the majority of other clubs, the fans would not be pleased with numerous players from their nearest rivals. Danny Butterfield had not been good enough for a mediocre Palace side, so why should he be good enough for us?

The only positive to come from the game was the return of Zheng from injury. Despite being one of the best players in the division, his return was far too late. He may have made a difference if he had not been injured. Pardew may even have kept his job. But with only ten games remaining, Zheng was no miracle worker.

Towards the end the away fans were singing 'That's why you're going down'. Of course one bad game was not why we were down, but the ninety minutes against Watford summed up the season. We had done well in parts but the defending was abysmal, and we could not hang on to a lead or even a point. As soon as Watford scored, the confidence drained from the players and we caved in.

For the third time in three years, we had been competing with Watford for either survival or a playoff place. The previous two years neither side really triumphed as Watford were awful in the playoffs. But this year they looked like surviving comfortably. Leaving the ground, I really despised Watford. They were nothing special, yet again they were the happier side leaving the ground. Their fans obviously revelled in their win. It was sickening.

When Watford were relegated with us, I was pleased they went down as they'd stolen the two points off us, particularly at the Valley when we fully deserved three points. Similarly in 2007–8 they got two points off Charlton but did not deserve any. To see them lose in the playoffs was pleasing as their style of football was not pretty to watch, and like us with Reid, the loss of Marlon King had a lasting effect.

Just like the aftermath of the Forest home defeat, it was hard not to look at the manager especially as his record was no better than Pardew's (or even Dowie's for that matter). However in my opinion, it was the players that had to have a hard look at themselves. In our two biggest games for a number of months/years, we needed the likes of Hudson, Ambrose and Sam to stand up and be counted. They went missing.

After playing badly and deservedly losing our must win home games, we played well at two of the promotion favourites. Away at Reading we deservedly got a draw, Bailey scoring again to carry on his excellent form. Reading's home form had not been good. They'd lost to a few of the sides near the bottom, which did help us but had kept hold of their top players even through the January window so would be there or thereabouts. A draw and a good performance did not help us but only highlighted the fact there was enough quality in the squad.

Phil Parkinson had recently been voted Readings greatest ever midfielder. They loved him at the Madejeski Stadium, certainly more than at Charlton. After his brief tenure at the club, it would take one helluva turnaround for our fans to hold him in such high regard but plenty of managers have recovered from poor starts at clubs.

Four days later at Wolves, again we played well against a top side. Wolves would deservedly win the title, but Charlton matched them all over the park and could have got something. We lost lose 2–1 with Chris Iwelumo typically scoring after a long drought. The defending was not too clever, and we missed Ward, who was ineligible. Holland again showed he did not have the attributes to play at centre back. However, there was plenty to be proud of. Elliot saved a penalty to carry on his personal good form. Zheng scored a great goal.

Rob Elliot had been superb since coming into the side and could in no way be faulted; even against Donny and Watford when we shipped a lot of goals, Elliot was not to blame. The penalty save was a fine save and even though Weaver did not do a lot wrong, if Elliot had been in the side earlier, we might not have conceded so many. Around November time, particularly on crosses, Weaver looked shaky. In games against Barnsley and Birmingham when goals were conceded from wide areas and set pieces, Elliot could have prevented heavy defeats.

Zheng had a lot of quality. In 2007–8 for much of the season he was one of our best players, and his loss was almost as big as that of Reid's. One of the baffling things about the Zheng's situation was he would be out of contract at the end of the season only two years after signing. Two million pounds is lot of money for any Championship club, so the fact that we spent so much money and then did not secure his services for longer is crazy.

Zheng was probably the one player in the squad who would attract a substantial transfer fee but would now leave on a free. This also begs the question: why did we not try to sell him in January when even a cut-price sale would be better than nothing? At the same time as he signed in 2007, we also signed Dean Sinclair from Barnet for a very small fee. He signed a three-year deal and has not really got near the side, but the one player who could play Premier League was not secured for long enough.

Our next home game against another side with promotion ambitions in Preston was a dismal game with very little action. Even though we did not lose, there was a lack of ambition and urgency from the players.

Towards the end it seemed we were happy with a draw. Our chief executive, Steve Waggott, in his programme column, talked of the effects of another relegation. After being relegated from the top flight the year before large increases in revenue, our second relegation would also come at the worst possible time as we'd lose the increased TV payments for Championship clubs from 2009, as if things were not bleak enough.

Phil Parkinson chose a negative 4–5–1 again, which was disappointing, and it took until thirteen minutes from time for another striker to be brought on. Darren Ambrose turned in another disappointing performance in the first half and was rightly replaced; surely this would be the last we'd see of him at the club.

There was an international break after the Preston game. Unlike the one in early October, which heralded possibly our best news for years, this break would be filled with negative stories about the club. These stories centred on some of the non-playing staff being made redundant due to dramatically reduced income. This was no real shock due to relegations and the climate but still signified the precarious state we were in. With Southampton's holding company being placed in administration, there was the increasing possibility we could find ourselves in a similar state.

There was also the news that we would sell our training ground. Again, this financially based, and even though the effect on the football would not be severe, questions were being raised about administration. Due to the loss of parachute payments, we would certainly have to make more cuts and the worry of points deductions was looming.

Southampton was our next game. Even though they had not been deducted any points, it was a must win for them due to their league position. Saints had tried to get as many fans to St Mary's as possible to raise income and atmosphere. Having been to St Mary's, I think the fans create a cracking atmosphere if the side is doing well. The year I went was when they were struggling in the league and had not yet won at their new home. On this day they finally won their first game at St Mary's at Charlton's expense. This was at the time when both sides had top-ten ambitions in the top tier with excellent managers and faced with League One.

Clubs such as Southampton and Leeds have struggled to cope after losing their parachute payments, so the fact that we could follow a similar road was now becoming more possible. Of course this raises the question about what the leagues should do to ensure clubs do not go out of business and protect lower division clubs. When you see players getting more than £100,000 a week at clubs like Manchester United but only a few miles away Stockport are struggling to pay their players and staff, it shows how big the gap is.

Luton are a prime example of how the Football League has failed to protect clubs. Luton, who have played in the top flight and have a rich history, have suffered three successive relegations. The last one from League Two only because of a ludicrous points ban. I am not an expert on clubs' finances and the regulations some clubs have broken, but whatever they have done, the punishments are too harsh on fans. When Luton were relegated in 2009, a fan on Sky, who'd followed Luton religiously for years, was reduced to tears due to their demise. He summed up how the league needs to re-evaluate who is being punished for rule breaking and clubs entering administration.

Rules that impose points deductions and therefore in some cases relegations take away from the actual game. In 2008 Leeds would have been promoted but for their deduction whilst in 2009 the League Two table would have had a very different look. In today's economic climate, there is the very real possibility that in 2009–0, unless the rules are rectified, clubs will be going out of business as well as the league tables being more about finances than points.

Against Southampton we turned in our best away performance of the season and won a thrilling game 3–2. Our quality was shown with the goals from the star midfielders: Shelvey, Racon and Bailey. Racon scored another marvellous goal whilst Bailey was now comfortably our top scorer. His move out to the left had improved his form, and his scoring return was remarkable considering we had not scored enough as a team. It appeared that come the end of the season, there would be some interest in the scorers, and we could have a job keeping them. Shelvey, who fortunately has signed a contract earlier in the season to mean we would demand a significant fee, had already been scouted by some top clubs.

With two games coming up in quick succession over Easter, our fate could mathematically be sealed. The first game was against second-in-the-table Birmingham. Amazingly despite the gap they, had scored only five more goals throughout the season than we had but obviously had a tremendous defensive record. They had an abundance of quality and a few ex-Charlton players, so it looked like an away banker.

Before the game the club released a promotional video celebrating the last twenty-five years at the club in order to persuade fans to renew their season tickets. The short film was quite moving as it showed the transformation of the club, the scenes when we returned to the Valley and the promotions. Obviously the film is supposed to be positive, and despite being about the last twenty-five years, it stops in 2005–6 as since then there had not been much to celebrate.

I will be renewing my ticket come what may, but the film was in some ways inspiring. To see how much the club has achieved and then seemingly has given away is astounding. I have talked about some of the famous wins, but the film shows some of the best as well as the Wembley win. Next season (09/10) we will be playing in front of small crowds in unglamorous venues when only a few years ago we won at places like Anfield and Stamford Bridge.

Charlton again played excellently and deserved a win. Brum keeper, Taylor, made at least two incredible saves whilst we also had a legitimate goal ruled out. Birmingham in truth looked like a potential Premiership side but then salvaged a draw after playing badly and would have better days. Hameur Bouazza returned and did not receive a favourable reception. Judging by his performance on the left, we had not really missed him as he was as trying as ever.

For this game I sat with Tom rather than in my usual seat. It was good to watch the game from a different perspective as well as with someone new. During the game we both agreed Kandol had been ineffective and was not the answer to our striking problems. Aside from chances on goal, we also created good opportunities to get the ball into the box, but Kandol was not good enough as his decision making was poor and at times was too slow in trying to make space and get himself into a positive position.

Also immensely frustrating was that again we had played well against one of the top sides. As in last season our record against the playoff hopefuls was decent. If we had raised our game against the sides we should have beaten, we would not be bottom. The draw meant, however, that we could be relegated on Easter Monday away at Coventry.

Our fate was not sealed against Coventry as another 0–0 kept us afloat. Again we were unlucky not to win as late on Bailey hit a post, but even six points from the Easter game would not have drastically changed things. We were twelve points from safety with only twelve to play for, so it would need a miracle.

In the lead-up to our next game, Parkinson came out and defended the loan signings. Understandably many fans had questioned the desire of these players. Some of Parkinson's loans had been successful. Ward in particular slotted in well, and with Wolves going up, he looked like a potential permanent signing. Still, players such as Butterfield and Gillespie had made no impact, so any criticism was fair. Of course when you have little money, loans are inevitable. But too many have underperformed, especially those who had done well in the Championship for other clubs.

Parkinson also addressed the striking options and the need for a natural goal scorer. He was right as we had not scored enough. Only Kandol had scored since December. Parky talked of signing Kandol permanently, which in my view would not be money well spent. Kandol had one or two good games but had scored only against Watford and did not look good enough. If we were going to spend money on a striker, there would be better options than someone who's average in the Championship and apparently in League One.

On 18 April Charlton were finally relegated. On a personal note, it was made worse that that day was my birthday. A month or so earlier the possibility became apparent that we'd be relegated on this day, and at least it added some light to the situation.

Even if we had won against Blackpool, it would not have made a difference as teams around us picked up points. But this relegation honestly hurt more than the one two years before. Of course again we fully deserved to go down and were the worst side, and yet again the players we had were good enough and had not done their job. When the whistle blew, this was the closest I have been to tears at a match. It had been such a long, hard season, and we had been the division's whipping boys.

Looking around the Valley when the whistle blew, I felt proud to support Charlton. Of course I was hurting, but already I could not wait for a new season and the chance for the players to right some of the wrongs. The fans had been superb all year, and although there were copious numbers of empty seats, my unconditional love for the club and desire to return in August had not changed.

In the game we were 2–0 late on thanks to Shelvey scoring again and Burton getting his first for Charlton from open play. At times Shelvey was a class apart and at seventeen continued to look the next big thing. However, some bad defending let them back into the game, and with virtually the last kick, their controversial striker Lee Hughes stole a point for the away side.

When the whistle blew and our fate was sealed, rather than boo the team and show our discontent at such a poor season, we applauded the players, which in some quarters seemed justified. Cynics say that players will never have the same passion as the fans have, but with the likes of Rob Elliot and Matt Holland, who looked close to tears, this is not always the case. Elliot in particular did not deserve to be part of a side bottom of the league. As a fan himself he must have been experiencing the same emotions as the home fans were.

This left nothing but a bit of pride to play for going in the last three games. First up against Cardiff there was a replica of the Blackpool game as we blew another 2–0 lead late on. Shelvey again scored a fine goal, but with little time remaining we were too naive and invited pressure. The defending again was not good enough as Cardiff's second goal scorer, Gyepes, was allowed to turn and shoot in the box.

A noticeable and not very pleasant thing about the Cardiff game was the number of empty seats, especially early on. Obviously since relegation from the Premiership, we had not reached capacity, but this game gave an indication of what the attendances may be like in League One. The official capacity was said to be 19,000, but it looked to be more like a cup game when the attendance would only be around 10,000–12,000, including a fair number from Cardiff. Looking around the ground, I was depressed to see so many empty seats and to think that so many people had seemingly given up and would not come back.

The same can be said of many other clubs who used to sell out, even in the Championship grounds, such as the Ricoh Arena. However, when these sides do well or even draw a big side in the cup, fans come out of nowhere claiming to have followed them for years. If Charlton do ever return, not that I will be complaining, there will be thousands who'll come back to the Valley every week, and maybe the cycle will start over again.

As I talked about at the start, some people believe that Charlton fans deserve everything they get. It was clear that against Cardiff the fans that gave us such a bad name had now gone. In this game and the previous one versus Blackpool, the home fans were singing 'Stand up if you're here next year'. These are the true fans of the club who will turn out every week in League One; the people who moaned at mediocrity in the Premiership probably did not even know who we were playing.

During the game the away fans came up with one of the funnier chants of the season, and even though it was at Charlton's expense, it still was amusing. They sang 'We're going to Wember–ley, you're going to Shrews–bury'. Four days after relegation was confirmed, I began to see the lighter side a little and as chants go, this was one of the more inventive.

At the end the team was rightly booed off, and there were chants of 'Parky out'. To give away two goals so late is unacceptable; for it to occur twice in a row invites criticism. This meant we were unbeaten in six but had won only one of these. If we'd won a couple more, at least we wouldn't have been so far adrift and some pride would have been restored.

The following weekend we lost at Derby in a game they needed to win to survive. Derby had appointed a new boss after Paul Jewell left. Nigel Clough had done a reasonable job considering they obviously were a club with severe problems following relegation. In the Derby team was Luke Varney, who'd continued to struggle for goals. He had done well in a loan away from Derby at Sheffield Wednesday but had not cemented a regular spot, and as when he was at Charlton, had often been used on the right.

The day after our player of the year was announced, Nicky Bailey was the favourite and deservedly won the award. Even though some would say in such a bad side no one deserves the acclaim, Bailey had been our best player and stood out. Already he was being linked with sides in the Championship and Birmingham, who'd be in the top flight. Shelvey and Racon had done well, but Bailey had been in the side for almost all of the season. Aside from his goal scoring, his overall contribution was significant. Bailey always gave 100 per cent and worked his socks off for the team, which was why he was such a fan favourite. Even when the team were not functioning, Bailey did his best to inspire the rest.

Parkinson said that if we had eleven Baileys, we would not be bottom. He was of course right. The midfield had not been the problem as we had players who most likely could do a job in the top flight. Zheng, Shelvey and even Racon are three of the best midfielders in the Championship, and Bailey was one of the highest midfield scorers, so there was a lot of quality. If the defence and strike force had similar strength, we could even have made the playoffs, as ridiculous as that sounds. Looking at the teams near the top, I think our midfield was as good as any.

Rob Elliot was second and like Bailey had a fine season. It was great to see Elliot do so well as he was a Charlton fan and had sat in the covered end as a youngster. He had expressed his hurt at the situation, and unlike others' his was genuine. Weaver was a terrific keeper, and you have to credit him for choosing Charlton after the history. But he was out of contract and most likely leave, so at least we knew that in Elliot there was a keeper capable of being first choice week in week out.

Before our last game of an awful season, two pieces of news came out of the club. The first was very significant: our academy was saved. There had been rumours we could not afford to maintain it, but after such success in youngsters coming through, the academy would play a vital role in the future. Since 2007 ten youth players had made their debuts. Of course some had gone on to be regulars and looked to be following players such as Fortune and Parker. One of the latest, Tamer Tuna, made his debut against Blackpool and following goals in the reserves and youth sides could get more of a chance.

With the likelihood there would be little money to spend and with our poor record with loans, our record of young players has been the one major success of the last few years, so it was a boost to know the set up would not be forced to shut.

When The Robin Stopped Bobbing

The second piece of news related to the release of a DVD package of highlights from the last two seasons. The decision to have such a DVD was criticised in the press, but for fans it is good to have season reviews. Even when we were relegated from the Premiership in '99 and '07, the compilation packages were still sold. Having got them at home, I have watched them back more than once. Also there have been some exciting games and great goals since '07, so it will be a worthy addition to the collection.

Our last game at home to Norwich was a massive game for the away side as they needed to win to stay up and hoped Barnsley lost. Like us they'd had a poor season, and their fans had many grievances with the players, former management and board. Bryan Gunn, who was a playing legend at the club, had not been able to improve things. But unlike Charlton's fans, their fans were generally in full support of their manager, and if they went down, he would not be held responsible.

A friend I met at university, James, was from Norwich, so going into the game we exchanged a lot of texts about how we'd be playing each other next year. He could not make the game, so I had to inform him of the goings-on. I am not sure he believed it when after thirty-odd minutes we were 3–0 up.

Bailey got his thirteenth of the season whilst Burton got two goals after awful defending. Watching Norwich and their fans reminded me of Charlton a few games before as the team really let down the away fans who'd come to London in their numbers. The defending at times was almost laughable, but you had to feel sorry for Norwich as they were going down without a fight.

Their fans were understandably very angry and voiced their displeasure at the players and especially the board. Like Charlton Norwich were not a League One side, and due to a number of circumstances had massively underachieved.

In the second half Burton scored his third to become the first Charlton player to score a hat trick since Kevin Lisbie almost six years before. Even though Norwich got a couple of goals either side of the break, our performance was top drawer, and Norwich could not cope with some of our quality. Even though it would have meant a loss for us, I would not have minded Norwich staying in the Championship. This is because as when we were competing with West Ham to survive in the Premiership, the feeling was out of the teams coming down with us. Norwich would have a better chance of bouncing back and would be competing with us more than Barnsley in League One would.

A comfortable win was, however, a win against a side that were not very good. Gary Doherty in their defence made ours look rock solid whilst in some areas Charlton surprisingly looked a class above. At the end our players actually got a standing ovation. Some of them deserved one, especially the younger players, such s Elliot and Shelvey, who since Christmas time had been excellent.

Darren Ward was taken off injured early against Norwich and was given a good send-off. It was likely we couldn't afford to keep him, but along with Sodje the year before, he had been probably our most successful loans. His replacement was another youth player, Chris Solly; he like many others fitted in well and would provide competition in League One at right back.

After the game in his post-match conference, Parkinson refused to discuss his future. No one knew whether he would keep his job, but Parky tried to stake a claim by saying the club needed stability. Fair enough. We needed continuity. But Parkinson had won only four of twenty-eight league games. Three of these wins had been against the three sides directly above us, so his record was unimpressive and this was the wrong time for Parkinson to stake his claim for the job.

After three summers of upheaval, the summer of 2009 will be another one. Let's hope the board and management will learn from their mistakes and try to ensure the club gets back where we belong. It had been one of the most disappointing seasons in our history; in many ways it was just a relief that the season had finished.

Chapter 13

DOING A LEICESTER?

It is too late to be bitter about our relegation from the Premiership. Of course it still hurts, particularly as since 2007 I have watched the season review as well as a DVD compilation with highlights from our top twenty Premiership games. This DVD shows how much we have lost, and seeing us beat Arsenal and Chelsea seems a lifetime ago. In our relegation season, many things went against us. With some more luck with players, managers and decisions, we'd have survived.

What makes it worse is that teams who survived at our expense as well as teams who are not as big as Charlton are doing well and have benefited greatly from the increased revenue. Teams such as Wigan and Fulham are spending more money than we ever did; they are spending it wisely whilst Charlton are not far away from administration.

Our second demotion, on the other hand, is one that we can still moan about and feel let down by. The players were undoubtedly good enough, and we should in no way have gone down. We may have been the worst side in the division, yet many teams who came to the Valley did not have to be at their best for their victory. In numerous games it was more that we underperformed rather than the other team playing exceptionally well.

There were teams who looked worse than we did, and at times our players looked superior. To go into a season with realistic playoff ambitions yet finish bottom certainly made Charlton the biggest flop of all four divisions. In August 2008, if you had asked the majority of fans their worst fear, it would have been another year of mid table mediocrity. Even the most pessimistic of fans would not have predicted a bottom-of-the-table finish.

When going through the games, I saw that a massive problem was surrendering leads and late goals. On far too many occasions, we would go ahead or draw level only to blow it. In any season you expect to surrender a lead and concede late goals on occasions, but in 2008–9 we lost a lot of points. If games finished after eighty minutes, we'd not have been bottom. Furthermore, throughout the whole season not on any occasion did we come from behind to win and rarely did we salvage anything after conceding the first goal.

The biggest goal we conceded throughout the year in 2006–7 was undoubtedly the Fulham equaliser; in 2008 it was the Derby equaliser. Both goals evoked the same emotions and looking back could have made such a difference. The two points gained would not have saved us, but a win on each occasion would have been major confidence boosters. In 2008 particularly, if we'd beaten Derby, Parky would have got his first win and maybe could've been a catalyst for a much better second half to the year.

In each of the three seasons, there are periods when it became apparent that we'd fail in our goals for the season. Of course there are individual games which made a difference, some certainly regarding managerial tenures, but there were spells which sealed our fate. These were spells where the players let the fans down and did not deliver when they needed to.

In the three Premiership games around Easter, we could have won but only drew (City, Reading and Sheffield United); these were for me the games where relegation was all but confirmed. This was because of the difficult upcoming games but also because in all three games we had the chances to win. Unquestionably in the home games, we should have done more to ensure the three points. Hindsight is obviously a wonderful thing, but if Charlton had been more adventurous going forward and taken a gamble, then who knows?

People who say that Alan Pardew had enough games to save us from the drop and should take some responsibility would look at these three games in particular. Certainly against Sheffield United a win would have given us a massive boos whilst making the away side's job a lot tougher. Even though it was United who went down with us, if Charlton had won, we'd have been competing more with the likes of West Ham and Wigan going into the final weekend rather than being out of the race.

The only other criticism of Pardew from this spell was the lack of firepower, which he could have changed by bringing someone in to help the half fit Darren Bent. We were willing to spend £2 million on Stokes, so when this move fell through, we should have looked elsewhere.

In the following season there is no dispute the sale of Reid was the major turning point; after he left we won only four more games. In some of these games, especially against teams nearer the bottom, his influence was greatly missed. Games against Blackpool away and Preston at home really killed the automatic hopes whilst the late defeat to Wolves and draw against Southampton put an end to the playoffs.

Against Wolves in particular after fighting back brilliantly, we should have taken the draw, but instead going gung ho cost us. If there was twenty minutes to go, going all out for a win would have been expected; but with less than a minute, the players should have been happy with salvaging the game.

In many ways this Championship season mirrored some of our seasons in the top flight when after good starts, we fell away during the spring and finished mid table. The major difference was before this was still not so bad, and the season would still be a triumph to be mid table. The loss of Reid certainly had more of an effect than the sale of Murphy did, but you could even say it was greater than the loss of Parker was when our European challenge ended.

Finally, last season two home games against Doncaster and Watford really killed our survival hopes. Before these games the task had been great enough, but successive home wins would've really given us hope and left us only four points from safety with a game in hand over the sides above. The performances in both games were not good enough, and we conceded very poor late goals. Individual errors are part of the game, but on far too many occasions they cost us vital points. If the players raised their games in the way the Charlton side did against Villa and West Ham in 2006–7, then similarly they'd have given us a fighting chance.

Both Doncaster and Watford stayed up fairly comfortably in the end but neither had to work hard for their victory; they did not win by out-playing or out-classing us. The away sides won because we were not good enough and our players went missing. Not saying that if our players had performed to the best of their ability we'd have got six points –as both sides we faced were decent – but there is no way we'd have lost twice.

The defeats left us with many games to play but not a lot to play for; we needed a massive miracle. Parkinson's tactics were too negative, and the players were not brave enough. There was a lack of urgency; at times it felt as though they had already accepted the inevitable. In both games we should have pressed for winners; instead we sat back and waited for the opposition to kill us off.

When searching for someone to blame for going from the brink of Europe to the Johnstone's Paint in a matter of years, it is apparent that many have contributed and no single body is wholly to blame. The players obviously have greatly contributed. But there has been such a high turnover since 2006, they are no way completely responsible.

There is no dispute that each manager has played his part. Dowie of course wasted a lot of money, which is still being felt today. To spend so much money is unforgivable and even though he may have had bad luck with injuries and referees, this does not hide the fact his spell was nothing short of a disaster.

Pardew has a decent first twelve months in charge and the situation he left us in was not irretrievable. Nevertheless he spent a lot of money, and some players flopped badly (loans and permanent signings). His team selection and tactics were questionable and if one word sums up his spell then it is inconsistency.

Similar to the spell that Pardew had in charge, I have mixed feelings about Parkinson's tenure. He had enough games in charge to save Charlton and some performances leave a very bitter taste. In terms of signings and team selection, he certainly did not learn from Pardew's mistakes yet in support of his, the club was in turmoil in November 2008. There were players with no confidence or belief that they could win a game.

Parkinson helped restore this to certain players and towards the end of the season, we had a side that looked capable of competing in the Championship. He also helped nurture some of the younger players and got the best out of players who had underperformed at times under Pardew.

There is also the feeling that maybe if Parkinson had taken charge before November 2008, he could have turned things around. What did not help his cause, was the Pardew association and the fact other clubs in the league were appointing managers from outside the club and reaping the rewards.

In my opinion the board that has to take the majority of the blame. Almost everything that has gone wrong at the club is down to their decisions, starting with the appointment of Dowie and sanctioning of so much money. I do not believe Dowie was the best candidate for the job, after the amazing job done before; his credentials were not impressive enough to believe he could handle the step-up.

Alan Curbishley in fifteen years never got anywhere near so much money to spend, yet Dowie, who hardly excelled at Palace with transfers, got £12 million after five minutes in charge. Surely someone on the board would have noticed that Dowie was buying players for too much money, players who were not going to improve the squad. When spending so much money, it would not have taken a board member long to seek advice that the money being paid was being wasted.

After putting so much faith in Dowie, they sacked him and went for the untried Les Reed, who was not ready for the job. The games he was in charge for, we may as well have written off. Reed had the best interests of the club at heart but was not up to the job and should not have been replaced as late as Christmas Eve. The board must have realised their mistakes and gone for the best candidate to replace Dowie, even if it meant spending more. With such a reward for top-flight survival, they took a massive risk with Reed.

In all fairness, the decision to bring in Alan Pardew was a popular one, and he seemed the right man to try to save us and if not, then bring us back. The board then did the right thing in backing Pardew all the way through to January 2008 when promotion looked a genuine possibility. The sanctioning of the Reid sale destroyed all the good work of the last year in building the club back up. They undermined Pardew and cost us promotion. To make matters worse, we were then forced to sell some of our best players in the summer of 2008 to make the task of bouncing back at the second attempt a lot harder.

The final major decision they made was to appoint Parkinson full time after he did not win any of his games as caretaker. It was a good idea to appoint a caretaker while the best man was found, but Richard Murray saying Parkinson was debatable and unpopular. Looking back however, a new man would in no way have guaranteed a turn around and Parkinson was hardly a complete no hoper.

There were plenty of good candidates, some out of work. As other sides have proved, a new manager is often more successful. Admittedly Norwich went down after sacking Roeder, but ask most of their fans and they'll say that's where they'd have gone anyway. Also as the last game of the season showed, their fans were in full support of Bryan Gunn. At Nottingham Forest and Watford, they both looked like following Charlton down, but their new managers proved very successful.

Of course when I talk of the board, my views are only opinions. I have no inside knowledge of boardroom politics and the individuals who have had a greater influence over the poor decisions that have been made. This may invalidate some of my arguments about the club and what has gone wrong, but I am sure if you ask the majority of Charlton supporters, they would agree that collectively the board has to take a large share of the responsibility for our demise.

Whilst there was no football to keep me occupied, I was away on holiday (still regularly checking the Internet, however, for updates). Normally when away as a football fan, you meet some fans of other clubs and discuss players, fans and such. This year I met some Sheffield Wednesday fans who were fairly knowledgeable about Charlton and immediately commented on Deon Burton and what a good player he will be in League One in 2009–0.

By all accounts Burton had a bad start to 2008–9 at Wednesday, which led to his sale. Before that had been impressive for them and was a firm fans' favourite. Having heard this and reflected more on the second half of the season, I think the criticism aimed at Burton has been a bit unfair and more reflective on the fact he was Parkinson's first signing and came into a side with no confidence or belief rather than his actual performances.

Unlike players such as Ambrose, Burton did not do a lot wrong and still brings a lot to the team; unfortunately the lack of goals until it was too late did not help his cause. Also he signed for the club just as Varney left. I believe Varney could have helped turn the situation around. If you ask the majority of fans who they'd rather have up front, Varney would win comfortably.

Next season is a clean slate, and Burton has a better goal ratio in League One, so one hopes he will prove to be an important player; certainly his experience should be valuable. The same applies to Matt Spring, who was a Parkinson signing but did not improve the team. Yet he has been there and done it in the third tier, so again the hope is he will be valuable.

Another Wednesday player connection is Nicky Weaver. All three times that he played against Wednesday he received an excellent reception, due to his being an avid Wednesday fan, and enjoyed a successful loan spell in 2006. The fans I spoke to said if they did not have Lee Grant and had more finances, he'd be welcomed back.

It was interesting to talk to some other fans that had seen their side go from the top flight to the third tier in a matter of years. The Wednesday fans said they hoped we'd come back. It took them two years, and they only sneaked up through the playoffs. It was also good to have some football banter and compete over what songs to request in a local bar (Wednesday fans wanted 'Hi Ho, Silver Lining'; we wanted 'Into the Valley').

As are Charlton's finances, Wednesday's are tight, and Brian Laws has done a fine job with no money. If we could try to replicate how Wednesday have got themselves back up and stabilised, we would not go far wrong (some investment would undoubtedly help though).

Despite all this criticism of the people in charge at Charlton, they have still done a hell of a lot for the club, and compared to many other sides remain one of the better. In the Premiership years they were second to none. Teams such as Newcastle, Southampton and even Leicester would crave for a board like ours and the stability we had until 2006. The board saved the club once before, and with any luck they will do the same again.

Even though we cannot afford to spend big on new players, if the board back the manager and are brave when negotiating over players leaving, this will build many bridges. It would be great to keep our top players. If so, I'm sure Charlton fans will pray that we overcome the January window as well.

Leicester City and Charlton are similar in size, and over the last ten to twelve years our fortunes have been similar. The similarity was noted by many people at Charlton when it became clear we'd be relegated around March 2009 when at the same time Leicester were well on course to win League One only a year after leaving the Championship themselves. Our manager and chief executive both pointed to the example in the match-day programme; however, what they failed to mention was that Leicester appointed a completely new manager after relegation.

During the late '90s under Martin O'Neill, Leicester were promoted to the top flight; whilst there they competed well and surpassed many expectations. Likewise, they upset the odds on many occasions and won at some of the top stadiums more than once. They won at Stamford Bridge and also got excellent results at places such as Old Trafford. In 1998, for example only a free kick in the ninety-fourth minute from David Beckham cost them a famous win.

O'Neill's management style is very similar to Alan Curbishley's. O'Neill had a reputation for finding bargains and successfully bringing through younger players, notably Emile Heskey who had one of the most successful periods of his career there. Since leaving Leicester, O'Neill went on to be one of Celtic's greatest bosses, winning a lot of silverware, and is now mounting a serious challenge to the top four. No doubt that given the right opportunity and backing, Curbs could go on and do an equally good job. At West Ham it was the right job but possibly the wrong time. If the fans and owners did not treat him in the way they did, they could be in Europe by now.

Unlike Charlton they even managed to reach a couple of cup finals and in 2000 won the League Cup. However, after O'Neill left they would not reach these heights again, despite yo-yoing between the top two divisions after relegation in 2004. In 2008 Leicester were relegated to League One, despite having a lot of quality players and Premiership resources, particularly their new stadium.

Even though they only just went down on the last day, there are obvious parallels in the two squads. For example their defensive record was amongst the best in the division. When they were relegated, some of their defenders were very sought after and jumped ship. Our defenders would not attract the same amount of interest as players such as Gareth McAuley but our midfield certainly would. Like Charlton, the Foxes could not put the ball in the net, and this was the main problem throughout the year as the strikers struggled greatly.

Leicester's decline took longer than Charlton's but was equally dramatic. When looking at their relegation in 2008, one can see they also had management issues and questionable board decisions. During the years both sides were in the top division, the press and pundits often referred to 'doing a Leicester or Charlton' when referring to promoted teams and their strategies.

Now teams getting promotion look at Wigan or Bolton as teams to follow. It is clear that it does not take much for teams to start falling. Bolton nearly got relegated when Sam Allardyce left, and it would not surprise me if they or another seemingly comfortable side follow Charlton or Leicester's path.

Many people pointed at the Leicester example after they were relegated because they found a new manager who stabilised the club. Nigel Pearson built a side with a low budget that was good enough to comfortably get promoted. Unlike our last two managers, Pearson utilised the loan market well and got the best out of the players who underperformed in the Championship.

When looking at the management structure at Leicester over the last few years, I think it has been at times more farcical than Charlton's. Unlike our board and chairman, Milan Mandaric at Leicester is notoriously hard to please and has chopped and changed his manager a lot. The season they were relegated they went through three permanent managers. But unlike at Charlton the manager who was in charge of the majority in Ian Holloway actually had a respectable record. He lost an average of only one in five, which is not relegation form, but too many draws due to lack of firepower cost them dearly.

With Holloway's record at his previous clubs, I would have thought he could have led Leicester to promotion but was not given the chance. As I have said, Holloway would have been ideal for Charlton but instead we went for the 'best man' for the job in Parkinson.

Even though both sides had some players capable of improving most Championship sides, one player who had radically improved in League One was Matt Fryatt, who benefited from managerial confidence and regular football. He scored bundles, including a couple of hat tricks, so the hope is some of our younger strikers who had not been regulars would be more suited to the third tier and could show the ability shown at previous clubs (McLeod, Dickson and the others).

Charlton's loan signings have been more miss than hit, but one noticeable difference between our loans and Leicester's was that they went for quality youngsters from top clubs who were not ready for regular top flight games but had enough quality to play for Leicester. Players

When The Robin Stopped Bobbing

such as Jack Hobbs and David Martin from Liverpool were amongst their best players in 2008–9. These players showed the sort of desire that we had missed; they had far more to prove and gain from a successful loan. Our loans tended to be players who were either not fully fit therefore needing game time or not first team regulars because they had not been good enough.

It is no coincidence that our more successful loans came to the club with the possibility they could sign permanently. If we could afford Darren Ward, he would be a great signing. Sam Sodje has also been linked with a return since he left us in 2008 and would be welcomed back.

An example of a side that have utilised the loan market well are Blackpool. For the last two seasons they have finished in respectable positions in the Championship. Blackpool have a small budget, but some of their loans, including DJ Campbell and Alan Gow, have been far more successful than Charlton's and have ensured they have survived.

Next season it would certainly be nice to have more of a stable squad rather than a new player making a debut every week. Understandably there will be short-term loans and youngsters coming through, but forty players playing in a season are far too many.

The final major reason to believe we could follow Leicester is the use of the younger players. Both sides have tremendous academies, and their younger players – particularly Andy King and Joe Mattock – played a major role in 2008–9. With our increased reliance on youth and the obvious talent there, looking at the Leicester model gives every Charlton fan great reason for optimism.

Leicester had, however, been one of many big clubs going down to the third tier; some sides that would be considered bigger had gone down before and not immediately bounced back. When looking at League One in 2009, I see the obvious one is Leeds, whose fall has probably been the most dramatic in football history.

In 2001 they were ninety minutes from a Champions League final yet only six years later were in danger of going down to League Two after being deducted fifteen points in League One. This deduction actually cost them a return to the second tier. After having some of Europe's brightest players, it makes Charlton's decline seem small as they enter a third consecutive season two divisions below the Promised Land.

In March 2003 Leeds were fighting relegation. They arrived at the Valley having sold some of their top players but maintained the likes of Robinson, Kewell and Viduka. This afternoon Leeds thrashed us 6–1. We were awful. Yet this afternoon with the talent in the away side, I firmly believe they would have beaten any side. Mark Viduka scored a fine hat trick. For one of the only times in the glory years we were demolished.

Even the year when they were relegated, the team that again won at the Valley had plenty of quality, including Smith, Viduka and Milner. Compared to the Charlton side of 2007, Leeds in 2004 probably on paper looked better odds to survive.

Like numerous others they have disproved the theory that there are sides too good to go down. Also like a lot of others, they have had been plenty of problems with managers and the directors. If it were not for the board at Leeds in the early 2000s, they would possibly still be in the top tier. Some of the decisions by Leeds board were thousands times worse than Charlton's. Our board have cost us status and money, yet at Elland Road, they nearly cost them their whole club.

Leeds will no doubt be competing with Charlton for promotion, but they have shown how tough it is, even with some good players. Similarly Nottingham Forest and Sheffield Wednesday also found it difficult after falling down; it took both sides two years and plenty of change, so if we did not already know it then, League One would be exceptionally difficult.

I think we have more of a chance getting promoted this time around than in 2007. The Championship is a lot harder to get out of as it is in some ways like a Premier League Two. Some big sides have come down whilst unfancied teams have got up. In 2009, who would have thought Newcastle and Burnley would swap leagues? In my opinion the second tier is among the most competitive leagues in Europe.

In 2007–8 there was more chance of Scunthorpe beating West Brom than Derby beating Manchester United. The teams at the top swapped round almost weekly, whereas in the top flight there was a huge gap between the top four and the rest. In terms of size Charlton are between a Premiership and Championship size; therefore, there was always a huge possibility we would be relegated and stay there for a few years as did Ipswich or Coventry before. Not in my worst nightmares did I envisage another unsuccessful relegation battle and our leaving the second tier from the bottom.

League One is slightly different. There are some quality sides, and teams have proved that by playing football on the ground rather than long ball can reap plenty of rewards. Teams such as Doncaster and Swansea have fantastic philosophies regarding the way they play and have recently proved you do not need to bully teams to win games outside the Premiership.

Swansea in particular adapted very well to the second tier and were unlucky not to get into the playoffs. Next season it will be hard for them to repeat the success due to their manager, Roberto Martinez, leaving for the top flight as well as potential departures of key players. Nevertheless, they got out of League One by playing attractive football and shrewd signings so like Leicester should be looked at as a model to replicate.

With Charlton's resources and infrastructure, for us not to be challenging things would have to go very wrong (we may have said this before though). There is going to be fierce competition, but with the right manager and some better signings, in a year's time we could look forward to Newcastle or Boro rather than Yeovil.

Our last promotion involved our scoring a lot of goals and rarely being tested; looking at the stats, one can see that we walked Division One for most of the year. It is very hopeful to believe the same will occur again. If we can find another Andy Hunt who scored twenty-four league goals and a defence which kept a record number of clean sheets, then who knows? Admittedly that year we spent some big money on Kiely (£1 million) and Svensson, and this would not happen again. But even back then the players who'd come through the academy played a vital role, especially Richard Rufus (one of the undisputed best defenders never to have played for England).

When The Robin Stopped Bobbing

At this time I cannot predict who will stay and go in terms of player or coaches. If Phil Parkinson stays, we have to forget the last season and hope the job he did at Colchester can be replicated. He made his reputation there when he took them up. With the greatest of respects to them, Charlton are much more fancied.

The fans will have to accept the board's decision no matter what and get behind the team; after all we all want the same thing. It will only take a few months of successful results for the fickle nature of fans to set in and opinions to change. We have to have faith in the board; up until three years ago they were faultless.

Unlike many other fans, I actually believe that Parkinson may be the best man for the job this time around. Like many I criticised and doubted his appointment yet he has handled the farce that has been Charlton Athletic with great dignity. He has stabilised the club and some players have excelled (Bailey, Racon etc).

Parkinson has been preparing for League 1 for a long while and has hopefully laid some good foundations for a successful season. Therefore a new regime would only move us backwards and would not guarantee promotion. Parkinson was spot on when he said the club is in desperate need of stability.

No fans want to keep moaning about their club. We don't want to go to the Valley every Saturday waiting for the team to fail so we can rant at the people in charge. We all want a Charlton that we can be proud of. For too long now when wearing replica shirts and telling people who I support, the response has been one of sympathy.

In terms of player news, as of late June 2009, high earners such as Weaver, Ambrose (who later signed for

Palace) and Todorov were released whilst Josh Wright left for Scunthorpe after not being offered a new deal. None of these were great losses, and to get players on possible Premiership wages off the bill was a relief as their contributions did not reflect their talents.

Even though none of these players was particularly favoured by the fans, I think Weaver especially deserves credit for signing for Charlton after his antics in 1999 and when he could have got potentially more money to sit on the bench at City. He came to the club to play regular football and in his first year was first class. Unfortunately a loss of confidence and form cost him, and even if we didn't have Elliot, I doubt Charlton could afford to keep him. Unlike some of the other departures, I hope Weaver gets a good club and does well.

The Josh Wright situation is a crazy one. According to reports we could not afford to renew his contract, so he left for free without the club receiving any compensation. Wright may have done well out on loan at Barnet and Gills but fell out with Parkinson and is no world beater, so to see him go albeit for nothing does not leave any sour tastes (unlike if other midfielders were to leave).

The club reported that Zheng Zhi, Holland Fortune and Randolph were to be offered deals, but no announcement has been made on whether they have accepted yet. Zheng will probably go as we may not be able to afford to offer a decent contract, and he is far too good for League One. If he'd stayed fit, maybe we would not be in League One. Wherever he ends up, I wish him all the best as well.

I would like to see Jon Fortune stay as at centre half. We have lacked depth in the last year. For someone who did well in the top flight, he should be one of League One's best. If Fortune leaves, he has shown good loyalty towards the club over the years, and it is hard to begrudge him a chance at a higher level. The other two will probably not be regulars, so to losing them would not be the worst news; keeping them would stop pointless loans or spending money needed elsewhere.

We have signed Miguel Llera from MK Dons on a free. Llera is a centre half. This looks like a good bit of business for the club as he did well in a side that narrowly missed out on promotion from League One and will surely be a regular next season.

This signing, however, paved the way for Mark Hudson to join Cardiff. Again this looks good business as a year ago we signed him on a free and have received an initial £1.075 million, which for a club in our financial position is a welcome boost. Hudson, like the players who were released, did not perform consistently enough to justify his reputation; and despite the fact Hudson was a good leader and was not one of the worst performers, for a million his loss won't be felt too hard.

Andy Gray remains our player but has been linked with a move away and like Hudson should command a decent fee. If given the right service, Gray should get upwards of fifteen goals in a Championship season but did not perform consistently enough for Charlton and would cause a mixed response if he left. In the third tier, Gray would certainly get towards twenty in League One, but the money we would receive is much needed when there are goals elsewhere in the squad.

Unfortunately some players who fans would love to have stay have attracted plenty of interest, and we may struggle to keep them, particularly the trio of Shelvey, Racon and Bailey. It would be great to keep all three. If we are serious about promotion, I think we need at least two to stay. Bailey's excellent form at the end of the season has alerted clubs, and Racon fitted in well after injuries to give our midfield balance and much needed quality. Both are still relatively young so could even play in the top flight one day.

Jonjo Shelvey has been linked with the Premiership; the hope is if he does go as well as a sizeable figure, which will help the club no end. He'll be loaned back to us for a year or two to continue his development. The chances are we will not be able to afford any substantial offers, but it would be good to see the board act bravely and hold out for as much as possible.

Crystal Palace had their own star, Jon Bostock, who was sold to Spurs in 2008 and has barely played. Both players have represented England at youth level, so maybe Shelvey will consider waiting a year or so before his big move. After all he is only going to get better and needs regular football.

An interesting idea would be for us to try to attract some of our old players from the glory years (1998–06) who are no longer good enough for the top two divisions but could do a great job in League One. Maybe it is being too nostalgic to think Chris Powell, Johansson and Kishishev would ever come back (if we could even afford them) and replicate the form that made them terrace favourites, but it is a nice thought at least. Chris Powell perhaps could join the coaching staff and take the first steps to be a manager.

There have been talks of a takeover, and Peter Varney, our ex-chief executive, has been mentioned as the man leading a consortium that will save the club and inject some much needed cash. On the message boards, there have been endless rumours from 'reliable sources regarding a new owner and potential new managers. We have seen Ian Holloway, Paul Ince and Jim Gannon all take new jobs despite being loosely linked with Charlton. However, as of June 2009, there has been nothing to convince fans these are anything more than rumours, yet!

All the same Charlton fans have been here before, and there is still the possibility of the opposite happening where the financial situation continues to worsen and we cannot afford any changes. No fan wants to think about administration, but it is a reality of modern-day lower-league football. Without any cash investment, the likelihood increases. In the current economic climate, football clubs do not look like the best investments, so any sort of takeover could take a fair amount of time to go through. It could be a long summer with many twists and turns.

Takeovers at clubs are not always as good as they seem and can cause even more chaos. At Newcastle the Mike Ashley takeover has not led to any progression. It is hardly likely that we are going to get our own Randy Lerner.

Now the season is behind us, I am immensely looking forward to a new season. It would be nice if people's predictions that 'at least we may win a few games now', comes true. Even though we are playing in the third tier for the first time in a very long time, there is still plenty to look forward to. There are new grounds to visit and new teams to see play. I would love to go to Carlisle, and having not visited Elland Road, this is a trip that I also look forward to.

There is the possibility of competing in the Johnstone's Paint Trophy and maybe even a first visit to the new Wembley for Charlton. Having seen other sides play there, I think it would be phenomenal to walk down Wembley way in a Charlton shirt celebrating a win and maybe a promotion. If we got to Wembley, the chances are we'd sell out our allocation. To be there with more than 30,000 other fans would be very special.

After three years away from the top flight. An away cup tie at a top-four side would be good, even if we got a hiding. A trip to Anfield or Old Trafford would be great. Even a home game against a big side would generate some much needed money for the club.

The fixtures were released in mid June. We will start at home against another promoted side in Wycombe (Oh dear. December 2006). Our first away trip is to Hartlepool as a real welcome to the third tier. And there are games against teams most would except to be near the top in Norwich and Leeds in the opening two months to make our start very interesting.

Notably there are more southern sides in League One than in the Championship, so away trips are easier to get to, especially around the festive period when we have a couple of London derbies. One away trip that is a little further from home is Carlisle, which is on a Saturday in October. I am disappointed this is not on a Tuesday night in bleak winter, but apparently it is still well worth the trip.

When The Robin Stopped Bobbing

Our traditional curtain raiser friendly at Welling United will be eagerly anticipated, as it is the first time we see the new players and a chance to focus properly on the coming season. Welling is even more local than Charlton for most fans, so there's normally a healthy Charlton following. There have been a few goals in previous games, including 8–0 and 5–1 Charlton wins.

Finally, I cannot wait to get back to the Valley and truly put the last seasons behind us. It has not even been that long since the Norwich game, but already I miss football. . It is nice for a week or two to not have to worry about the weekend game, but as a fan you never stop. If it is not about the next game, it is about players being sold. Close seasons are exciting for transfers and summer tournaments but little else.

The events of the last three years will take a lot of repairing; there have been a lot of lows and few highs. However, one good season and a return to the Championship will go a long way to restore faith. The second tier is still a good division to be in with plenty of terrific sides. Since 2006 it has not been a happy Valley, but watching old DVDs does rekindle some astonishing memories when the ground was full up and buzzing.

By the time Wycombe arrive at the Valley, all the optimism and hope will return no matter who the owners and players are. There will be another nine months when we go through the same emotions all over again, minus the pain I hope. One excellent win and we'll believe we can win the league, yet a couple of defeats and it will be the same story. Fans are fickle, but no matter what we'll be back and will never give up hope.

Daniel Macionis

Realistically without a lot of money, it could be a while before we're back to the levels of 1998–2006 but we have fallen very quickly, so maybe Charlton can rise just as fast again and the next chapter of Charlton's modern history will be a successful one.

June 2009

Lightning Source UK Ltd.
Milton Keynes UK
30 September 2010

160592UK00001B/5/P